'Full of spirit, candour and good sense ... provocative in all kinds of ways' *Telegraph*

'It's a real joy to see young women taking up feminism in such positive ways' *Herald*

'Refreshing and eye-opening and much-needed ... *I Call Myself a Feminist* might be specifically targeted at younger women but readers of any age stand to learn a whole lot from this anthology' Katie Grant, *Independent*

'There are many chapters here that enlighten, cheer, or rightly anger. Some have real style and swagger ... the best are often those that refract wider social questions through the prism of personal experience ... *I Call Myself a Feminist* provides a lively and heartfelt introduction to many of the flash points of feminism, and manages to be both relatable and inspirational' *Independent on Sunday*

I CALL MYSELF A FEMINIST

Edited by Victoria Pepe, Rachel Holmes,
Amy Annette, Alice Stride, Martha Mosse

virago

VIRAGO

First published in Great Britain in 2015 by Virago Press
This paperback edition first published in Great Britain in 2016 by Virago Press

5 7 9 10 8 6 4

Essay Copyright and Acknowledgements on p261-69

A CIP catalogue record for this book is available from the British Library.

ISBN 978-0-349-00845-5

Typeset in Bembo by M Rules
Printed and bound in Great Britain by
Clays Ltd, St Ives plc

Papers used by Virago are from well-managed forests and other responsible sources.

Virago Press
An imprint of
Little, Brown Book Group
Carmelite House
50 Victoria Embankment
London EC4Y 0DZ

An Hachette UK Company
www.hachette.co.uk

www.virago.co.uk

To all those who call themselves feminists –
whether they say it out loud or not.

CONTENTS

INTRODUCTION

Amy Annette, Martha Mosse and Alice Stride

Some people might argue that we have reached Peak Feminism. That feminism has jumped the shark. That they are fatigued by feminism. They don't want to hear about it any more. 'How can we need more of it? It's already bloody everywhere – we've done it now, right? It's always on Twitter. Like, ALWAYS. I just want to eat my sausage rolls and watch *House of Cards* in peace.'

We know that being a feminist can feel exhausting, like trying to climb a mountain dragging a suitcase made of lead whilst wearing flip-flops. We all know that life was – perhaps – a little simpler before we became feminists. Ignorance is bliss, and dancing on bars IS fun – as Emer O'Toole reflected in her *Guardian* article 'Ten things feminism has ruined for me'.

But we also know right down to the marrow in our

bones that we need feminism. It is as necessary as oxygen. It is as essential as water and we gasp for it in the same way when confronted with sexism. It might be the grotesque out-and-out sexism that feels shockingly like a previously unseen football to the side of your head landing with a thwock, 'THIS IS CLEARLY SEXISM!' Or it might be the imperceptible sexism; the less obvious, less naked kind. The kind that you know is there humming in the background like a fly that will not be swatted. Thus we need feminism.

We need feminism because girls are shot in the head for going to school. We need feminism because women are burned alive for refusing to submit to grotesque male desires. We need feminism because women are under-represented in every sphere of life except being wives and mothers. We need feminism because one in five women in the UK experiences sexual violence and is usually blamed and shamed for it. We need feminism because we are taxed for our bodily functions. We need feminism because women's bodies remain politicised, scrutinised, fetishised. There are countless more reasons why we need feminism, infinitely more reasons; and this in itself is another reason that we need feminism.

We know that many young women and men need feminism too. We need to feel included, engaged and inspired to fight for an equal society and an equal world. This is an exciting time to be a young feminist. The world pulses with feminism – a feminist fairground, all bright lights and toffee apples. It seems cool, vibrant, sexy to be a feminist. We have access to ideas and resources and thoughts and articles that feminists in the seventies could only dream about and we have a mind-boggling, accessible platform to shout about it from – the internet. We have allies the world over, and feminism is no longer seen only as a 'women's issue'.

So, when Lisa Appignanesi, Lennie Goodings, Rachel Holmes and Susie Orbach invited us to help create a book, we said 'YES.' The time felt right, and we knew there was an appetite for a book like this, due to the success of their 2013 book *Fifty Shades of Feminism*, to which Alice contributed with her essay 'Saving the Bush'. (Her sister has finally forgiven her for writing publicly about her pubic hair.) But this time, the contributors would all be under the age of thirty. We wanted to champion the young feminist. We wanted to know what this generation has to say: the generation whose only unifier might be that each person has an identity as unique as our Twitter handles.

This book would not be for any certain 'type' of young feminist. It had to be all-inclusive – like the crap holiday you went on when you were eighteen with your friends from school, from which you came back with rum and cola for blood and a new-found talent for 'tactical vomiting'. Our wonderful contributors, these extraordinary women – some of them still teenagers! – are dazzling. They all possess distinct and exciting voices and backgrounds and sensibilities: a smorgasbord of fantastic young women and their superb ideas. We've covered all sorts of interesting stuff, and it has come from a brilliant array of perspectives. The hijab! Feminist scientists! Feminism and religion! Fat feminism! Language and sexism! Sex! The self! Suffragettes!

We knew immediately what we wanted this book to BE like. Choosing a name proved much more difficult. If this book were a human, it would have been known as 'The Baby' for the first six months of its life. So why did we title this book *I Call Myself a Feminist*? Because this book is for everyone everywhere – a statement of intent. 'I call myself a feminist' is an active, personal and powerful phrase. It is a statement of a way of thinking that we have chosen to become part of us – a part of the many quirks and intrigue that make us ourselves. We are not born a feminist; we become one. This sense of ownership is important: the term 'feminist' remains under siege, cast aside for being too inclusive and broad, and there are many who refuse to identify with it. We are challenging this with *I Call Myself a Feminist*.

We hope that there is something in here for everyone who reads this book. We hope that there is at least one essay that makes your stomach churn and your heart beat faster in recognition. We hope that you'll want to thrust it in front of your friends and family and bellow: 'THIS! This is exactly what I have been trying to say! I get this!'

We felt rallied together by this experience, the experience of making a book – together as editors, and with all of our splendid contributors – and we are all united by feminism. We know that young feminists are out there in droves. We ARE you. This one's for you. This one's for us.

[We] need to reclaim the word 'feminism'. We need the word 'feminism' back real bad. When statistics come in saying that only 29 per cent of American women would describe themselves as feminist – and only 42 per cent of British women – I used to think, What do you think feminism IS, ladies? What part of 'liberation for women' is not for you? Is it freedom to vote? The right not to be owned by the man you marry? The campaign for equal pay? 'Vogue' by Madonna? Jeans? Did all that good shit GET ON YOUR NERVES? Or were you just DRUNK AT THE TIME OF THE SURVEY?

Caitlin Moran, How to Be a Woman

My coach said I ran like a girl, and I said if he ran a little faster he could too.

Mia Hamm

Whatever you choose, however many roads you travel, I hope that you choose not to be a lady. I hope you will find some way to break the rules and make a little trouble out there. And I also hope that you will choose to make some of that trouble on behalf of women.

Nora Ephron

GOOD FOR A GIRL ISN'T GOOD ENOUGH

Hajar J. Woodland

I'm going to write this like a man. I could agonise over making it perfect, worrying about how to justify myself to every reader, or I could simply put across my opinion and write it to a standard that's good enough.

Even now, in the twenty-first century, working like a man has positive connotations. Competent, rational, confident, to the point. Like a woman? Although advertising campaigns might seek to redefine the term, it's still used as an insult. Writing like a woman? Long-winded, emotional, unsound.

I envy men who possess the self-assuredness and authority that mean they're surprised when they're unable to perform tasks or solve problems. The men for whom 'Let me take a look at that for you, darling' soon becomes 'a design flaw'. It's not usually down to sexism, but rather an innate sense of competence they're equipped with thanks to thousands of years of role models, problem solvers and experts.

Raised as a rare breed of white British, half-Iranian, practising Sunni Muslim, I grew up believing a man's opinion was more valuable than a woman's; that a man could make decisions and answer to God on my behalf. While I spent much of my early twenties trying to understand and overcome the religious obstacles of my upbringing, it has only been in the last five years that I have started to bring my own inner misogynist to task. The fluffy, clumsy, irresponsible child within who's happy with the validation that comes from being either a good girl or 'good for a girl'. This girly girl – let's call her Bob – believes in the limitations of the female brain. She's the reason I might add a smiley face to soften the blow of a serious email, or doubt my own abilities, opinions and decisions. Bob can go fuck herself.

Damaging comparisons between boys and girls start young and school is where we cement the idea that there are fields we simply don't expect girls to excel in. A well-intentioned maths teacher was one of the first to make me aware that I was 'good for a girl', coming third in my Year 9 exams. Just knowing that I wasn't expected to be as good as the boys made being 'good for a girl' good enough. I knew

I could attribute any failings to my gender rather than to not enough hard work.

When my six-year-old niece happily donned a sheriff's hat for the school's 'Wear a Hat Day', several parents at the event commented on how it was an unusual choice for a girl. However harmless the odd remark might seem, over time such responses to a girl's choices and interests could easily weaken her resolve to lead the life she chooses and might discourage her from pursuing her passions. Teachers and parents have the power to eradicate language that is detrimental to girls and young women. It was a feminist teacher who first challenged my belief in the superiority and advanced wisdom of men, after I suggested that she ask one of the boys in the class to help her fix the television. Another feminist teacher talked in depth to us about victim-blaming and rape culture. By the time I left school these strong women had helped me make the first small steps towards questioning my beliefs and inner misogyny.

'Good for a girl' is so often offered as a compliment, yet it is in fact a free pass to failure and mediocrity. Good for a girl gets us the validation we're told to seek, so why try harder? If one doesn't succeed in matching the men, there's always beauty, marriage and kids. Call it competitiveness or bravado, or perhaps societal pressure, but for men, ineptitude is rarely linked to gender. They might well get 'sensitive for a boy' or 'good at knitting for a boy', but these perceived limitations don't impact the global landscape in the same way. Being 'good for a boy' at sewing hasn't prevented men from becoming world leaders or CEOs in the same way being 'good for a girl' at economics has affected women's access to these positions. Studies have demonstrated that women perform worse when they are told that expectations are low. At school, the idea that we're 'good for girls' is injurious to both our success and our self-esteem, and if unchallenged, it continues into and negatively impacts our careers.

In the workplace, feminism is armour. Several years ago, before starting an assignment for a client, I mentally prepared myself to go into the role working like a man. I made it very clear that I was a feminist from the beginning, and it took a lot of determination not to cave in to Bob when I battled my desire to please and be approved of for making cups of tea. In meetings I tried to cut to the chase and be assertive when I felt time was being wasted. I would make no bones about calling a man out when he was mansplaining. Although I believed in this new persona, my feminist intuition wasn't always strong and feminism was the rational angel on my shoulder asking me 'Is this fair?' or 'Would you do this if you were a man?' – and occasionally punching Bob.

These feminist beliefs gave me the confidence to respond 'Yes, boy' to a colleague who insisted on calling me 'girl' at every meeting. My principles forced me back to my seat when I rose to make colleagues tea just so that they might like me. It wasn't about the beverages but about ensuring I wasn't perceived as servile. Feminism reminds me that I don't need to make an open display of maternal characteristics just to make my personality more acceptable.

The words 'I don't make coffee', at a Women in Investment Banking event, have most shaped how I try to view myself professionally. When asked how she would react to fellow professionals asking her to get refreshments, a senior VP said she would firmly state 'I don't make coffee.' Resounding in my head with her American twang, this is still such a powerful phrase and represents how women could position themselves in the workplace. We are not powerless before men. We do not have to do as we're told. We can be shamelessly strong and refuse to make the coffee. In order to recognise external barriers, we must first understand those we put up ourselves and challenge our own misogyny. We must challenge the accepted traditions and undermining comments that we don't always stand up to for fear of seeming troublesome or unlikeable; the additional unpaid hours of the office homemaker – the woman who waters the plants, books meeting rooms, makes the tea, smiles and laughs at everyday sexism for fear she might be seen as uptight or unfriendly. We can only go so far with global human rights and equality issues while we still see ourselves – no matter how subtly – as inferior to men. The lack of women in boardrooms isn't a more pressing issue than violence against women, but we cannot tackle one successfully if we do not stand against the injustice of the other.

I believe that it is in our professional lives that we can make the biggest steps for both men and women. We may never truly overcome the demons of our upbringings or the gender inequalities we face outside the office, but in industry we can legislate for change, and support women in their successes. We can craft an ideal to aspire to that could filter out into other aspects of our lives.

Working like a man is not just about external perception. In my work as a copywriter, it helps me to silence my inner critic. I remind myself to be less afraid of people's opinions, to send assertive emails that don't sugar-coat difficult conversations, and to work quicker instead of trying to make every last word perfect. In writing this piece, though – which involved an all-nighter at three words a minute and three Hobnobs an hour – I was struck with a severe lack of confidence. I was writing what I believed in, but the question that surfaced above all others was 'Why does your voice matter?' I felt that what I was writing couldn't possibly make sense and so I sent the unfinished draft to my editors, hoping they'd get my point. I was relieved at the praise it received but I knew that my doubt hadn't been the false modesty or insecurity of a writer – it was my inner critic doubting the validity of my opinions. I know that silencing my inner misogynist will take time. It's not a lightning bolt that will change the world in an instant but a daily top-down habit that starts in the mind and that I hope will become instinct. My voice might not always sound as strong or as cogent as I'd like on the first attempt, but I know that the more I speak, the quieter Bob will get.

From a shy, somewhat melancholy girl I became, before I was nineteen, a self-confident woman who could hold crowds of thousands ... All I wanted was a piece of chalk and a 'lorry' [low, flat wagon] because I was too small to speak off a soap box and all by myself I could rouse any district ...

Sometimes, my meetings began in a very rowdy fashion; mobs of boys and men would gather round the box or chair on which I was mounted and pelt me well with eggs and tomatoes or over-ripe oranges, but I generally met them with good enough humo[u]r to win their silence and I would end up by having an enthusiastic hearing. I am and always was incapable of thinking out a joke beforehand, but sometimes I saw, quite spontaneously, the humorous side of things, which was very helpful with an obstreperous crowd. Once, I remember in Bradford, I had a particularly tiresome narkish interjector, who eyed me sourly, from under a lamp post, and kept up a running fire of disparaging interjections; at last he said: 'If you were my wife I'd give you a dose of poison'. No need of that, my friend,' I replied cheerfully, 'If I were your wife I'd take it'. The audience yelled with delight and my tormentor left the meeting early.

Adela Pankhurst

If you don't understand, ask questions. If you're uncomfortable about asking questions, say you are uncomfortable about asking questions and then ask anyway. It's easy to tell when a question is coming from a good place. Then listen some more. Sometimes people just want to feel heard. Here's to possibilities of friendship and connection and understanding.

Chimamanda Ngozi Adichie, Americanah

HOW COULD I NOT BE?

Laura Pankhurst

My great-grandmother, Sylvia Pankhurst, was the same age as I am now when she, her mother Emmeline and her sister Christabel formed the Women's Social and Political Union. The WSPU, nicknamed the Suffragettes, began in Manchester over a century ago – a tiny group of women made up of the Pankhursts and a few of their friends. But what they became, and the story of their struggle before women were finally allowed to vote on equal terms with men, in 1928, is now taught in schools up and down the country.

I'm often asked what impact my surname has on my life. I like to think that I would be engaged in socio-political issues whatever surname I was born with, but there is no doubt my name has far-reaching effects on me. There are photographs of me as a baby with my mum, Helen Pankhurst, in front of the statue of Emmeline outside the Houses of Parliament; of a five-year-old me with my mum in front of a 'Votes for Women' banner; and of my mum and me at a panoply of women's rights events ever since. These photos and markers of my childhood are snapshots of the wider context of women's rights-related activism that I have been lucky enough to be involved in.

For the last few years I have been leading CARE International's Walk In Her Shoes Campaign on International Women's Day together with my mum and the 'Olympic Suffragettes' – a group of fantastic women involved in the 2012 Olympics opening ceremony who have since been campaigning on a variety of issues. The aim of Walk In Her Shoes is to honour the past, celebrate achievements and to unite in solidarity with on-going women's rights concerns, and in particular to highlight the fact that in many parts of the world women still face unacceptable poverty, inequality and injustice. The walk is a wonderful way to make sure that the single day of celebrations is linked to fundraising and personal commitments around development activism.

Our events have gathered pace, and we are now linked to more and more feminist activists, including young social media activists, female and male. Speakers have included politicians from the main parties, as well as comedian Sandi Toksvig, Laura Bates (founder of the Everyday Sexism

Project), Lucy-Anne Holmes (founder of No More Page 3) and Somali women's rights activist Zenab Abdirahman, to name but a few. The growing sense of common purpose, nationally and internationally, between activists and the wider public is fantastic to witness. So is the revival of interest in the Suffragettes, partly linked to the May 2015 general election and the film *Suffragette*, directed by Sarah Gavron.

This side of being a feminist – being involved in events, combining traditional and modern social-networking-based activism, supporting very specific local single-issue-based campaigns and linking these up to international ones – feels incredibly positive. But no one can doubt that there is still much to do, in so many areas, to build a more inclusive and enabling society here and abroad, as well as to prevent a loss of what we have already achieved.

But what of this word 'feminism'? For me, a feminist is someone who believes in the need to fight for the social, political and economic equality of the sexes. And yet many people do not want to associate themselves with the term and use it disparagingly. However, if you put aside the word 'feminism' and talk about the ideas that it represents, most people agree with the principles involved and believe in the importance of fighting for equality. A truly depressing number of times, I have heard women and men say they are not feminists because they have a narrow and derogatory image of what the term epitomises. Many individuals who are in fact politically active, who sign petitions and worry about issues such as violence against women, still – even with this raised consciousness about feminism – shy away from the term. Once we start talking and break down what a feminist is, i.e. someone who believes in equality and equal opportunity, and who believes that there is still a lot to be done to achieve this, almost everybody ends up – however reluctantly – agreeing that they are in fact feminists.

Sure, there are anti-feminists out there who would prefer to put the clock back to days when there was a greater sexual division of work and a more patriarchal hierarchy, but from my experience, these are a shrinking minority. More numerous are those who are slightly scared of the term, scared to stand up and be counted – especially in a world which is increasingly against the dichotomy and simplicity of labels. This is problematic because, for as long as there is still work to do in terms of addressing gender inequality, we will need people who self-identify as feminists and who wear the term as a badge of honour, a reminder of the need to speak out and contribute to the tide of change.

I am a feminist and I am a Pankhurst. I am incredibly proud of both of these facts. I am also aware of the privilege of being a descendant of women who have stamped their mark on history in a powerful and positive way. And in this, I am far from being alone. Many people come up to me and share the pride they have in a grandmother or great-aunt or even occasionally a great-grandfather who was a Suffragette or Suffragette supporter. Since Emmeline and her fellow Suffragettes started campaigning, there have been four new generations of Pankhursts involved in social and political activism around women's rights. How many more generations, I wonder, will be needed to fight on until gender inequality is confined to its appropriate place in the history books?

In my own case, I had to train myself out of that phony smile, which is like a nervous tic on every teenage girl. And this meant that I smiled rarely, for in truth, when it came down to real smiling, I had less to smile about. My 'dream' action for the women's liberation movement: a smile boycott, at which declaration all women would instantly abandon their 'pleasing' smiles, henceforth smiling only when something pleased them.

Shulamith Firestone, The Dialectic of Sex

If you retain nothing else, always remember the most important Rule of Beauty. 'Who cares?'

Tina Fey, Bossypants

If you obey all the rules, you miss all the fun.

Katharine Hepburn

MY JOURNEY TO FEMINISM

Louise O'Neill

I was fifteen when I first used the F-word. It's difficult now, when the biggest female popstars in the world proudly call themselves feminists, to explain how alone that made me feel. I didn't have an online community such as Rookie or Jezebel or xoJane to reassure me that there were other girls out there who felt the same as I did; all I had was a tattered copy of *The Handmaid's Tale* by Margaret Atwood and Hole's *Live Through This*, and I held them close to my heart like a talisman.

Being a feminist in 2000 was not cool. Friends told me that Courtney Love was crazy and that everyone knew that Kurt Cobain had really written *Live Through This*. They said feminists burned their bras, hated men, and believed that all forms of sex were rape.

I tried to become more informed, taking modules in gender and sexuality studies at university, reading Germaine Greer and Hélène Cixous and Susan Faludi, and although I did become increasingly confident about proclaiming myself a feminist, it is clear to me now that I still didn't understand what it meant.

Here are some things that I did in my teens and early twenties, while still identifying as a feminist.

- While identifying as a feminist, I was the human embodiment of the Cool Girl/Manic Pixie Dream Girl. I was determined to seem easy-going and relaxed. Nothing fazed me. I didn't want to be one of 'those girls' who were demanding and high maintenance and needy.
- While identifying as a feminist, I said things like 'Don't be such a girl,' and 'Girls are bitches, I prefer hanging out with guys, there's less drama.'
- While identifying as a feminist, I believed the media when they said that false claims of rape were common and that men's lives were ruined by it.
- While identifying as a feminist, I went home with a boy. I told him to stop, and he kept going. He tore my legs and my heart apart, but afterwards I said nothing. I told myself it was my fault. I had been drinking. I had been wearing a short skirt. I had gone to his bedroom. I had been asking for it.

- While identifying as a feminist, I enforced strict gender roles with my boyfriend, expecting him to pay for our meals and to take care of me emotionally. If he expected that support in return, I somehow felt that made him 'less of a man'.
- While identifying as a feminist, I starved myself and made myself vomit after meals in order to satisfy an idea of what I thought an attractive woman should look like.

I called myself a feminist, but in truth I was buying into the patriarchy. I was internalising all of that misogyny, making it my own, making it my truth, and I didn't even realise it.

I would like to tell you that it's easier these days, but I have to admit that it's still not completely innate. The manacles of a lifetime of cultural conditioning that has tried to convince me that gender is a biological fact rather than a social construct are more difficult to shake off than I would like.

At a friend's wedding, the groom choked up during his speech and I felt uncomfortable. A girlfriend called someone the C-word and I thought, 'That's not very ladylike.' After a particularly gruelling therapy session I had a fight with my mother for failing to take care of me after a family member had died when I was fourteen, and my father said, 'Why didn't you expect me to take care of you?' The answer came far too quickly – because he was only my father. I expected my mother to nurture me, to be *better*, simply because she was the woman.

And we do that, don't we? We hold women up to a higher moral standard, we tell them to be nice, to protect their virginity, to be the gatekeepers. We expect them to be 'good girls'.

That's why I wrote *Only Ever Yours*. I wrote it because I felt tired. I wrote it because I felt intrinsically ashamed of the parts of myself that made me female. I wrote it because I felt a bit broken. I wrote it because I wanted to start a conversation about how we see and treat women.

This is what feminism is about. It's not about witch covens or misandry or drinking Male Tears (as fun as all those things sound). It's about equality. It is about creating a world where gender stereotypes don't weigh heavily on either men or women or anyone in between, where we are all free to be ourselves without recrimination for failing to conform to a certain idea of what masculinity or femininity represents.

So come with me, teenage girl. Let me hold your hand. Let us say it together.

'I am a woman. I am a feminist. And I am proud to be both.'

This article first appeared on the *Guardian*'s children's and teen site on 21 January 2015

Find out who you are and figure out what you believe in. Even if it's different from what your neighbors believe in and different from what your parents believe in. Stay true to yourself. Have your own opinion. Don't worry about what people say about you or think about you. Let the naysayers nay. They will eventually grow tired of naying.

Ellen DeGeneres, Seriously … I'm kidding

As long as you keep a person down, some part of you has to be down there to hold him down, so it means you cannot soar as you otherwise might.

Marian Anderson

HOTSPUR: SUPERWOMAN

Jade Anouka

In 2014 I was honoured to be cast in Phyllida Lloyd's production of *Henry IV* at the Donmar Warehouse. Two years earlier I'd been in *Julius Caesar* playing Calpurnia, Metellus Cimber and Pindarus, in the first of what will become a trilogy. The final all-female Shakespeare is yet to be announced. I was eager to again be part of work that promoted women in theatre and challenged ideas. Eager to get my mouth around Hotspur's words. Those words that were usually reserved for men. Oh, it felt good!

Playing Hotspur showed me what I wanted to be as an actor: to be free on stage. I could be strong, get angry, punch things, be funny, fight, use charm, commandeer; all things you rarely get to do as a female actor and I relished the moment. When I was Hotspur I felt like a superwoman.

There's a moment during the play when I and two others do pull-ups while in the middle of a conversation. Every night without fail we'd walk up to the bars and begin, and would hear the audience gasp. I'm sure there were many reasons for the audible reaction at this point in the production but the sound, for me, underscored a moment of recognition: three women working out on stage is just not something you see. After the shows many women commented that 'my husband couldn't even do that' and that they wanted to start training and doing boxing classes so they could get fit. A friend of mine crafted a new saying, 'strong is the new skinny'. It just felt great to show the boys we can do it too, that we don't have to be limited to watching and admiring their attempts. And all this in a packed-out theatre in London's West End; it was an incredible feeling to be part of something that felt important, on so many levels. I trained for this work, in schools, in fields, in gyms, in the ring, and here I was playing a character who felt sexy in her oversized grey tracksuit and Reebok Classics that were so comfortable and enabled me to drop down and do ten … press-ups, sit-ups, dips, jabs, whatever. We had no make-up and in some cases shaved heads. We weren't pretty; beautiful, yes, but not what many grow up thinking a woman should be. We weren't men either, we were women speaking text and being given the freedom to command a stage in a way I had never had chance to before. It was liberating! Yes, Hotspur was written as male, but I didn't think to play a man – I just tried to tell his story, play his actions, his way. Hotspur was sure, he never apologised for the way he spoke, looked, fought, loved, and when I played the part I felt a kind of invincibility. I could do anything a man could do *and* what a woman could too.

We took the production to Mulberry School, an all-girls comprehensive in east London. It proved to be an enriching experience. I was excited to talk to the girls and hear just how much the production affected them. Many said they felt 'inspired', like there were things they thought they couldn't do that they were now realising weren't just reserved for boys, they could aspire to do those things too. I recall in a post-show Q&A a teenage boy commenting how 'you never see this many women on stage'. When asked how he felt about it he replied 'I liked it' with a grin. He had a point, though: what we usually see on stage, what has become the 'norm', is lots of men with the odd woman thrown in. Now sometimes these female roles are brilliant. I've been lucky to play some fantastic ones: Olivia, Juliet, Ophelia and the wonderful Rosa in *Moon on a Rainbow Shawl*. But although they were great experiences, it's not enough. As an actor you always want more; as a female actor there needs to be more.

By doing an all-female *Henry IV* it gave women a

chance to play the kinds of roles that are not otherwise available to us. All-female productions are insightful, rare and exciting, and I feel they are also necessary to redress the balance on our stages until a time comes when we have equal representation across the board. Then we can all really play! Our all-female cast showed how rare it is to see women, lots of women, on stage, to see women in these big muscular leading roles, to see women be their own person, not just in relation to a man – and it also highlighted the misogynistic language that otherwise we, as an audience, often miss or disregard as the 'norm'. When Hotpsur's words 'I know you wise, but yet no farther wise / Than Harry Percy's wife; constant you are / But yet a woman', or Northumberland's 'Why, what a wasp-stung and impatient fool / Art thou to break into this woman's mood' come out of women's mouths, you notice the denigration in a more potent way.

I would jump at the chance to play Hotspur again. I would jump at the chance to be in an all-female production again. I would just jump at the chance to play an interesting, affecting, challenging role, male or female. What actor wouldn't?

Long may it continue that people like Phyllida Lloyd and places like the Donmar put on productions like *Henry IV*; likewise the many other people and theatres all across the country really pushing the boundaries of what's acceptable and challenging people's outdated, misjudged, preconceived 'norm' of what women can do. I want to live in a world where women are represented and regarded equally with men – and I want to work in one too.

The thing women have yet to learn is nobody gives you power. You just take it.

Roseanne Barr

What we can remember when we look at the past is that social change is always possible, and when an idea grips sufficient numbers of people, then it is inevitable. Despite all the disappointments of the last few years, there is no reason to give up hope or to stop believing that one day the future we desire could become the present we inhabit. There is no need to think we must start from scratch; the feminist foundations in our society are strong. We can be aware of and grateful for previous feminist successes while building upon them towards a better future. Because the dream that feminists first spoke about over two hundred years ago is still urging us on, the dream that one day women and men will be able to work and love side by side, freely, without the constraints of restrictive traditions. This dream tells us that rather than modelling themselves on the plastic charm of a pink and smiling doll, women can aim to realise their full human potential.

Natasha Walter, Living Dolls

It is very important to know who you are. To make decisions. To show who you are.

Malala Yousafzai

STAND UP AND GET INVOLVED

Emily Benn

Being maddened by the disproportionate impact of the actions of a tiny minority, and the example of a good mother: these are the reasons I call myself a feminist.

I should say first that I have been incredibly fortunate in my life, with an amazing education, supportive family and great opportunities. The same cannot be said for millions of women in Britain and the world today.

Looking back, it was at university that I first began to identify myself as a feminist. I graduated from Oxford University in 2011, and I loved almost every moment of my three years of student life. But when I properly reflect upon that time, there were tell-tale signs of casual, everyday sexism – 'lad culture' – that would rear its head again once I entered both politics and the working world.

At the time we all just went along with it. Talking to some of my contemporaries now – male and female – we still ask ourselves why we didn't do anything to try to stop the lewd conduct and derogatory chatter aimed at women from male fellow students. Partly, we didn't want to be known as kill-joys, but more importantly, we didn't realise how leaving this unchecked could lead to a bigger problem in the years ahead. And it is a problem.

While it never put me off standing up and getting involved, the undeniable effect of just this tiny minority's behaviour has been to crowd out too many women's voices, as many were put off full participation in university life by what they saw and were unwilling to put themselves in the firing line. This lad culture is a growing issue (I would urge you to read Baroness Amos for more; herself a pioneering national and international politican, with a career fighting for women at the UN she is working with the National Union of Students to tackle the growing problem of 'laddism' on campus) – and one which many brave female students across Britain are exposing and fighting. I'm proud to call myself a feminist alongside them.

I now work on the trading floor of an investment bank – as you can imagine, quite a male-dominated environment. Not enough women join this industry – no doubt too many are put off by what are often outdated stereotypes – and so their talent and potential is wasted. Too many still leave prematurely.

No industry will survive in the long term if it continues to miss out on such a huge pool of experience and budding success. This is not unique to banking – too many businesses and industries are missing out on different perspectives and ways of thinking; a 'diversity of thought'. I really believe better decisions are made when you have a variety of voices contributing – male and female, and of different ethnicities and backgrounds. That's what feminism is determined to achieve.

What these experiences have taught me is that having strong male leadership – alongside women's – is absolutely critical if you are ever going to advance the cause of gender equality. I am fortunate to be working with some pioneering male colleagues who have shown great leadership and consequently helped us make significant progress. They recognise that they too need to be proud to call themselves feminists. Equality is all too commonly seen just as a 'women's issue' alone – the preserve of women-only networks and groups, as a side-line to the main business. It is not; it is just as important for male colleagues as for female – and absolutely central to the success of the business.

So far I haven't let those minority voices stop me from putting my head above the parapet and getting involved in political life. People often assume it is just because of my last name – my grandfather was the MP Tony Benn – but this couldn't be further from the truth. If anything, seeing my family's experiences and sacrifices up close should have put me off. I am just the type of person who, when they get angry about something – and I get incredibly angry about injustice in all its forms, sexism included – is unable to sit around and complain. I want to get involved and change things, and politics is a way to make real and lasting changes – my family have certainly shown me that. Complaining alone achieves nothing, and neither does cynicism.

It is not always easy, though. Campaigning on the doorstep – as I did every weekend (and many evenings) for months leading up to the general election after I was selected as the Labour candidate for Croydon South, in my home borough – can often be pretty depressing. There were long hours juggling a job, occasional public abuse and the knowledge that I was likely going to lose (I was contesting a safe Conservative seat). But if you believe in something strongly enough (in my case, in a fairer economy, better housing and education, and in everyone enjoying the opportunities I have had) you should stand up and fight everywhere, not just where you'll win. And losing only makes you hungrier to succeed, and keep going.

Was it any different being a woman, and a young woman at that? Many people when I was out campaigning automatically assumed it was the men in the group who were leading the campaign and went to talk to them first. And I certainly got more comments about my clothes, looks, hair, you name it, than any of my male colleagues, some of them hardly flattering – it seems it's acceptable to say whatever you like if you're talking to a politician in the street. Again, this kind of scrutiny reserved for women (when did you last read any comment, flattering or otherwise, about a male candidate's clothes or appearance?) is enough to put off many of my female friends from getting actively involved. Such candidates as I owe a great deal to the many pioneering women politicians before us for setting such a great example of how to persevere and deal with these things. I did get a couple of marriage proposals, though – sadly neither of them particularly suitable.

I look to my family in India to see how things can change against all the odds. Here it is certainly the women who are making the weather and who are the breadwinners: succeeding in many industries – education, technology, law – breaking down barriers along the way. And we can all see how much richer their communities and families are as a result. They are the luckier ones, though. Meeting just some of the women across India who are suffering on an unimaginable scale is an experience that will stay with me for ever (I urge you to support the Women in India Trust if you can). The potential of that great country would be multiplied several times over were every woman given the chance to succeed.

And finally, I am sure a lot of women would, when asked for their feminist inspiration, go straight to their mothers. I am no exception. I have been blessed with wonderful parents. My mother, who settled in England as a child after living with her grandparents in India, battled some real experiences of racism in 1960s suburban London, working her way up through university to end up working for the

Prime Minister in Downing Street (via living with David Bowie and singing on his albums – she is far cooler than I am). The way she has recently battled and beaten cancer illustrates her trademark resilience, optimism and courage – classic attributes for so many inspirational women.

But above all else, my mother and my father, taught me two things. Firstly: don't let the bastards get you down (so applicable to that tiny minority discussed at the beginning). But more importantly, if you believe in yourself and really work hard enough, as hard as you can, then you can achieve anything you set your mind to. Just think what incredible things we would see if every young girl growing up around the world was encouraged to feel the same.

The F-word is Fairness.

Kate Mosse

For me, being a woman suits what I want to talk about and what my audience wants to hear.

Maybe I'm a dying breed.

Jenny Eclair

A male acquaintance of mine, with whom I have never had a dalliance, said to me, 'You know what? If you lost a couple of stone ...'

I said, 'The rest of this better be a fucking equation.'

'If you lost a couple of stone, we could probably go out.'

I said, 'Only if the couple of stone I lost was my fucking head.'

Sarah Millican

It is better to be alone, she figures, than to be with someone who can't see who you are. It is better to lead than to follow. It is better to speak up than stay silent. It is better to open doors than to shut them on people.

She will not be simple and sweet. She will not be what people tell her to be.

E. Lockhart, The Disreputable History of Frankie Landau-Banks

WHY I AM A FEMINIST

Sofie Hagen

I hate women. You know the ones. Those skinny, blonde women who know nothing about football and talk about shoes all the time. They are everywhere as well. On billboards, on TV, in all my favourite sitcoms, in every music video. Every stand-up comedian on TV talks about them as well – often with anger and annoyance. I completely connect with that – those women sound incredibly annoying. So I hate them too.

I can hate women because I am not one. I am *one of the guys*. I always have been. There came a point growing up when we all knew we had to make a decision. We were no longer children; we were either little men or little women. I looked to my mother for guidance on how to be a little woman, but she just stood in front of me wearing clothes from the men's section in our local supermarket; the closest her face had ever come to make-up was a little stain of paint from when she single-handedly painted our entire house; her shoes were cheap trainers, worn down from long shifts at the factory; and her pose was manly, arms folded and feet firmly placed on the floor. No angles in her body, a brick. She rolled her eyes when I asked if it was time for us to buy me a bra – and then sat me down to watch another Nicolas Cage action movie with her. The other girls in my class had received guidance – and soon we split up. They became little women and I became one of the guys.

You are never truly one of the guys. No one ever tells you that. No one ever told me to be careful – because no matter how many headshots you are able to kill with in *Counter-Strike*, you are never anything but a girl. Michael fell in love with me first. Then Morten. Tom never fell in love with me, or maybe he just never said it – because our two friends had beat him to it. I was furious that I could not just be one of the guys, that suddenly I had to think about how to be a woman again. I intensified my male behaviour: I skipped class, I burped, I talked loudly and often about porn. All to remind them to not fall in love with me – for I was a friend, not a *girl*. I dated Michael for a while and gave Morten his first kiss. I did not fit into the new box, *girl*friend. So I left.

I was *one of the guys* in high school as well. Except there it was just me. I protested everything and I protested it loudly. The drunk biology teacher who graded us by throwing a dice. The curtains that had not been changed since 1985. The overpriced carrots in the cafeteria. The students they gave a two-week detention – and nothing else – for attempting to rape another student. She left the school. They graduated and they are smiling in their class photo.

I was told to arch my back, smile and do my homework like a *good girl. Stop trying to get attention*, I was told. It is very unflattering. I did not stop protesting till they threatened to kick me out of the school. I wanted to stay. My masculine energy was helping me get to Louise, a beautiful redhead who only wore sweatpants and hoodies. She cared about handball and nothing else. I thought we would be *one of the guys* together. *Two of the guys*. She was the reason I rigged a drinking game, just so I could kiss her. When we returned to school after the summer vacation, she was wearing heels and make-up. I should have been upset but instead I was jealous of how quickly she had learned to become a woman. I then started hating even her, for caving in, for becoming what I could not be.

After high school, I met Ina. She was not a woman either. She did once buy fifty pairs of shoes in one day, but they were all in sizes way too small for her, as she was handing them out to orphans in Saint-Louis in Senegal. She does boss men around, like the women on TV, but only because she is the leader of the fundraising department of one of the biggest charity organisations in Denmark. She does not know the offside rule though. Typical *women*.

I met Eva. Eva was not a woman either. Not just because she had a tendency to sleep with them every once in a while, but because she was always a rock. To me and to everyone around her. I know of men who cried on her shoulder. She cut her hair short. She sat like a man would, with spread legs and shoulders raised, as if she was always ready for a battle. Which I think she always was. I believe her shoes were always dirty and had holes in them. I never found out if she knew anything about football, because we were always busy discussing homelessness or mental health.

I moved in next door to Michelle. Michelle is not a real woman, far from it. Michelle drinks like a man, burps like a man and speaks like a man might after spending a year at sea. When a guy tried to stick his finger into her anus on the dance floor, she turned around and smacked him so hard across the face that he fell to the floor. Later, she made sure he was fired from his job. Real women do not do that, real women do not cause scenes like that. Arch your back, shut up, Michelle.

Ida was not a woman. I once saw her drink a can of beer from a straw – through her nose. And Ane, Ane always complains that her boyfriend does not want to have sex as often as Ane does. Sanne has chosen not to shave her pubic hair. Lucy is afraid of commitment but her boyfriend wants marriage and kids. Amy puts squeaky toys in her bra so it makes a noise when she honks it. Then she laughs for hours.

I am still one of the guys. The guys being this layered, diversified, strong, opinionated, colourful, extraordinary palette of women I never see represented on TV or in other media. In 1994, when we had to choose if we wanted to be little women or little men, they should have been up there on the billboards. There are currently two types of women: the woman on the billboards and the women who grow up feeling wrong. I was twenty-five years old when I realised that I did not hate women. I do not even hate the woman on the billboard. I hate that the possibility of not being her, of not being a Barbie doll, was hidden from me. I hate that I was never given the opportunity to embrace *my version* of womanhood. The womanhood that is inclusive of all kinds of women. We need that. That is why I am a feminist.

If you are always trying to be normal, you will never know how amazing you can be.

Maya Angelou, Rainbow in the Cloud

We are taught that we must both blend in and stand out – a contradictory message indeed.

Susie Orbach, Fat is A Feminist Issue

Sex can be art. Look at Björk's *Vespertine*, a highly sexual and sensual record by a woman entirely in charge of her career and sex. The same can be said about almost every Prince record, and should be. Both are artists, adults and human beings, intelligently addressing a human subject, not exclusively a male one …

If Rihanna had not grown up watching the videos of the nineties, then it might not be quite so essential for her to portray her sexuality so luridly, so constantly and so influentially on the next generation. If the power was taken away from sex in pop by making it harder for younger viewers to access it, then maybe the focus would shift to making works of artistic beauty and conscience. And fundamentally that would actually be putting the power back in sex for a future world where women are able to portray their sexuality as it is for them.

Charlotte Church

SILENT SCREAMERS

Yas Necati

I know, from being in a school less than two years ago, that schoolkids give a shit. Most of the time they're wrapped up in trying to fit somewhere and not seem too weird, but they give a shit. Even if they pretend they don't.

But for too long young people have been let down by a mainstream media that makes out we're opinionless, schools that treat us like cattle and a government that ignores our voices altogether.

Some of us label ourselves to get by – others bitterly reject labels. We're fighting each other instead of uniting and fighting back against the people who got us into this mess in the first place.

I was one of the ones who picked a label to get by. Feminist.

I was seen as The Feminist. Bra-burning, man-hating, angry, feminazi, extreme, radical, unapproachable, easily picked on.

I was really a feminist. Let down, discontent, ready to scream, and make biscuits, cat-loving, queer, gender non-conforming, hippy.

I feel like a part of something bigger since I've become a feminist – but it wasn't always that way. School is a hard place to be a feminist because we as young people are tearing each other apart because of our differences. And I was seen as different.

Thinking about feminists, there were the artists and the writers, but they all seemed so different from me, and completely inaccessible. I knew no other *real-life* feminists, let alone *real-life teenage* feminists. Feminism seemed to me like some weird alien cult that existed in theory, but no everyday person was genuinely a part of it. Feminists were all either a lot older, incredibly academic or already dead. I was none of those things. I was a confused schoolkid worrying about her GCSE exams.

After a few months of feeling completely alone, I was relieved and perhaps a little too over-excited to 'discover' that my old English teacher was a *real-life* feminist. She used to call out sexist jokes in the classroom, and she prioritised an education in respect for others over the curriculum any time. I thought she was awesome; I still do. But she was an adult, and I was fifteen. I thought teens didn't care – I was wrong.

Of course, there were others who were interested. There were many more who were definitely feminists, but didn't identify with the label. Since my days as a fifteen-year-old student, I've had the awesome experience of meeting – and becoming good friends with – some of the coolest people I know: many, many feminist teenagers. Teenagers who are campaigning and advocating for gender equality, creatively and with fierce passion. I once thought that I was the only one who cared, and I now see myself as naive for thinking so. But many other young people have said that they felt the same way to start with. Luckily for all of us, there is a whole movement of teenage feminists doing incredibly powerful things. Whether you're one of us already, or just starting out, you're not alone. You're awesome.

The thing is, feminism can be isolating at times. Feminists are often isolated from the people around them, for believing in something as controversial as equality. And as teen feminists, we can feel isolated within the feminist movement itself, for being a bit younger than everyone else! Feminism is still very adult-centric, and often leaves behind young people's voices. I'm not calling for a teen-centric feminism, I'm calling for a feminism for everybody. If adults are going to be having fun out on protests, singing flashmobs and making change, then teens should have a chance to get involved too! If adults are having discussions about equality, teens should always have a say too. So let's start here.

There are loads of factors that play into people not being listened to – gender is one of many. Race, class, disability, sexual orientation, sexuality all have an effect on how we as people are represented in society. I'm going to focus on gender here – but issues of sexism don't exist inside a bubble: they intersect with many other inequalities, and it's important to remember that.

Sexism towards women is rife – and this includes trans women, and gender non-conforming people in general. Some men are assigned the gender identity of male at birth and identify as male – these men are really lucky, because they don't face discrimination on the grounds of their gender like the rest of us do. If we're sticking with labels, the technical term for these lucky men is 'cis-male'. 'Cis', meaning gender-conforming. Anyone who doesn't conform to the gender they were assigned at birth is 'trans': people who know they are the opposite gender to their birth-assignment, both genders, or no gender at all (and there's a whole spectrum of gender identities, so I wouldn't limit it to these – this is a very simplified explanation for something that is far from simple: identity).

Gender non-conforming people and women both face sexism in society – but I am by no means saying that we experience it in the same way. However, we do have one thing in common: we are not cis-males, and this means we get the short straw. Our voices are left out, we're always treated as less important and we have to work twice as hard to get anywhere. We are also bloody bold and brilliant. Many of us are activists – so why does nobody ever hear about us?

I mentioned earlier that there were plenty of people in my school who were plainly feminist, but wouldn't ever say so. And this is where mainstream media are at fault. In the *Sun*, the *Star*, the *Daily Mail* ... we get represented every day as if our opinions are insignificant. Young people get represented every day as opinionless, naive and not worth listening to. When you take both of these groups and put them together – when you combine 'young' and 'non-cis-male' – you realise that we're mostly under-represented and almost always misrepresented.

This more often than not discourages young people from politics, particularly if we're not cis-guys. We see it as something that's distant, confusing and not for us. We're less likely to share our opinions because we know we won't be listened to and we fear that we'll be mocked. Young women and trans youth feel we know that nobody will take us seriously. So most of the time we just don't say anything.

I speak out because I feel I have to. Because I look at the level of injustice and inequality in society and I know things have to change. I wasn't inspired by academics – I was inspired by artists and poets and musicians and friends. And I know there's a whole movement of young people now coming together. Because we're fucking powerful.

I'm fed up with female and gender non-conforming

teenagers being silenced because mainstream media, wider society and the feminist movement itself are telling us we shouldn't have a voice. Let's scream so loud they have to listen. Let's stop muting teen activists and start listening to them. Because we have just as much to say as anyone.

This happened late one night when I was on my way home after a party:

A man came up to me and said, 'Excuse me, madam.'

And that made me happy, because everyone called me 'sir' those days.

Only then he started to apologise. 'You should kick me right up the arse,' he said.

And at first I didn't understand.

But then I knew: he was seeing me as a man now. And the worst insult one man can give another is to call him a woman.

And that's why I'm a feminist.

These days men often open doors for me. When they speak to me, it's in a condescending way, as if I'm half witted.

It's strange. No one ever used to talk to me that way. Do I look stupid all of a sudden?

No. It's not that. It's just I look like a woman.

And that's why I'm a feminist.

Last month I saw four men in suits walking towards me. I could feel them look me up and down. Appraising me.

And they all thought the same thing at the same time:

Old. Fat. No good in bed.
Doesn't exist.
And their eyes went right through me and they passed on.
And that's why I'm a feminist.

But I do exist. I do belong to half the human race.

And after so long being disempowered and silenced we are finding our power and speaking with our voice.

Wherever that happens, the world gets better.

And that's why I'm a feminist.

Jo Clifford

There were plenty of feminists on TV in the early nineties, and I always sided with these tough ladies, the ones that didn't see men as their superiors. Raised by my mum, my gran and my aunty and bullied by a father I despised, child me was certain that women couldn't be the inferior gender. Teenage me wondered why there even had to be an inferior gender – or, in fact, gender at all. Couldn't we all just do our own thing and be nice to each other? At college, most people thought feminist meant 'man-hater'. This excluded men from feminism, including me, because, at the time, I looked like a boy.

It was a figurative kick in the teeth being born male – but when I was younger, I also got actual kicks in the face for 'acting girly'. Feminists have long fought to protect women from violence and I wish more of those with big platforms would discuss the very real abuse trans people suffer, often daily.

Early into my transition, I read Germaine Greer's *The Whole Woman*. It contained polemics about trans women in female toilets; suggesting we were men pretending to be women, trying to invade women's spaces. It's good to read authors one disagrees with. Greer caused me to question my identity, and form a more complex one. She was right: I am not a woman in the way my mother is; I haven't experienced female childhood; I don't menstruate. I won't give birth. Yes, I have no idea what it feels like to be another woman – but nor do I know what it feels like to be another man. How can anyone know what it feels like to be anyone but themselves? Strangely, thanks to Greer, I now know that I am happiest as me.

I do feel sorry for some of the feminist old guard, though. That fire they had in their bellies, that righteous indignation … it must be a shock to find they've joined the ranks of a chattering establishment, complicit in the oppression of others. I'm sure they never planned it.

I'm trans and feminist. Most of my female friends in their twenties are feminist too, though few call it that. We see ourselves as equal to others, even if they don't. We struggle to earn the same as our male peers, to be heard as much, to see as much of ourselves in public and political life. But we've progressed, through feminism and the idea that people should be treated equally despite what fate pops between your legs at birth. Who wouldn't support that? As Dale Spender so eloquently puts it:

> *'Feminism has fought no wars. It has killed no opponents. It has set up no concentration camps, starved no enemies, and practised no cruelties … Its battles have been for education, for the vote, for better working*

conditions, for safety on the streets, for childcare, for social welfare, for rape crisis clinics, women's refuges, reforms in the laws. If someone says, "Oh, I'm not a feminist!" I ask, "Why? What's your problem?"'

Well, here's the thing. The trans movement, fuelled by the radical notion that trans people are valid humans, hasn't fought any wars either. No killing. No concentration camps. Our battles are for dignity, not to be ridiculed, abused, and murdered for who we are; to have our privacy respected by the media, to be free from harassment under the law; free to use the toilet – free to pee.

Paris Lees

I believe that transgender people, including those who have transitioned, are living out real, authentic lives. Those lives should be celebrated, not questioned. Their health-care decisions should be theirs and theirs alone to make …

Obviously, there is much similarity among the challenges of transgender people and all women – from health care to harassment to discrimination in the workplace. And there is always the basic patriarchal bias against any sexual expression that can't end in conception, which is why kids on campus are sometimes mystified by the fact that the same groups oppose both, say, contraception and lesbians. I also think we have a lot to learn from original cultures that often didn't even have 'he' and 'she' in their languages, taught girls how to control their own fertility, and routinely accepted and had special roles for the 'twin-spirited'. These facts may remind us that patriarchy, racism, and nationalism have been dominant for less than five per cent of human history. Maybe they are an experiment that failed.

I know we've all worked hard on and are celebrating the Supreme Court marriage rulings this spring, but there is so much work to do to reach full LGBT equality – and ensuring that transgender people also have equality under the law has been the most left out and therefore should become foremost on that list . . . As feminists know, power over our own minds and bodies comes first.

Together, we are learning the deepest lesson. Families are not about form but content. Humans are not ranked; we are linked.

Gloria Steinem

There's just as many different kinds of feminism as there are women in the world.

Kathleen Hanna

MANIFESTO FOR FEMINIST INTERSECTIONALITY

Jinan Younis

> *When we don't pay attention to the margins, when we don't acknowledge the intersection, where the places of power overlap, we not only fail to see the women who fall between our movements, sometimes we pit our movements against each other.*
>
> KIMBERLÉ CRENSHAW

The theory of intersectionality was first developed by the feminist academic Kimberlé Crenshaw in 1989. She used intersectionality as a way to explain how black women experienced both racism and sexism, and how that impacted on their lives as women and therefore on the way that they engaged in feminism. The theory proposes that different forms of oppression, such as racism, sexism, homophobia, transphobia, ableism and classism, do not work in isolation. Instead, they meet, cross over and sometimes reinforce each other. People often experience more than one type of discrimination at a time, and need to fight a battle on many fronts. An intersectional feminist approach strives to take into account the many battles a woman may be fighting simultaneously with her fight against sexism.

Intersectionality entails working considerately with other women who have different experiences from your own and recognising the ways in which we might benefit from a system that disproportionately advantages some people over others. If we understand that, although we may feel completely disadvantaged by one form of oppression, such as sexism, we may still be the perpetrators of a different form of oppression, such as racism, then we can begin to forge strong relationships of solidarity with *all* women. As Audre Lorde states, 'I am not free while any woman is unfree, even when her shackles are very different from my own.'

Feminism is a movement led primarily by women for women. I, for example, am an Asian woman. I'm active in feminist movements and am keen on creating solidarity between women. Yet in many feminist spaces I feel as though my Asian and my feminist identities must be kept separate.

I have listened to women describe the hijab as 'oppressive', and I have never once mentioned in feminist spaces that when I was younger I used to proudly wear the hijab. Nor do I mention why I stopped – for fear of playing into a hugely negative stereotype surrounding Muslim women and their 'oppression'. As an Asian woman raised in a Muslim household I experience religious conflict and racism. As a young woman in UK society I experience daily catcalls and insidious rape culture. As a young Asian woman in UK society, I experience all of these things – often simultaneously.

It is crucial that feminist spaces are accommodating rather than hostile to difference. Ignoring differences means erasing the experiences of certain women, usually those that are most marginalised in our society.

This is true for the interaction between gender, sexuality and feminism. The need to accommodate lesbian, bisexual and trans women in the mainstream feminist movement is crucial, particularly as there are very few services that cater for LBT women across the UK, and the current cuts to domestic violence services severely affect LBT victims.

This oppression is often most harshly experienced at the intersection of race and sexuality. Black and ethnic minority women who also identify as LBT face not only homophobia/transphobia and sexism but also racism. In many cases, the families and communities of black and

ethnic minority women are the support
fight against racism, and yet these same
be the biggest barriers against LBT wo
terms with their identity.

In Cambridge University, the Black and Minority Ethnic (BME) branch of the Student Union's Women's Campaign (2015) ran a campaign called 'Ain't I a woman?' The campaign hosted a series of conversations with self-defining BME women about their experience of the university. One particularly striking conversation was with an anonymous BME student. She described her inability to find a place for *her* – a bisexual woman of colour who cannot reveal her identity because she worries about being ostracised from the safe spaces she has created for herself. She ended with a powerful statement: 'Queer black women need spaces too.'

She may have faced oppression on racist, sexist and homophobic grounds. These oppressions cannot be dealt with separately and neatly merged at the end. It must be recognised that this woman's experiences as a black queer woman will be different to the experiences of a white queer woman in the context of a racist and homophobic society.

An example of mainstream media being *forced* to listen to the lived experiences of women is the Focus E15 Mothers' Campaign. This campaign was formed by a group of single mothers who were facing eviction from their homes and, according to a piece in the *Guardian* in December 2014, it has 'done more than perhaps any other campaign group this

..o force social housing up the political agenda'. They ,attled against years of media demonisation of young, single mothers in order to get their story out.

Relevant feminism must take into account the effects of austerity measures and cuts, which disproportionately affect underprivileged women. We need to support *all* women if we want true liberation. Prioritising the voices of the less privileged will help address the imbalance created by a society which privileges those that are white, able-bodied, cisgendered (those who associate with the gender assigned to them at birth), straight and middle class. The *Guardian* columnist and head of the MsUnderstood Partnership Carlene Firmin intends to hand over her *Guardian* column to a young person at the end of 2015. Allowing those who are under-represented to have their own platform and to take up leadership positions is a way of redressing the balance.

Through intersectional feminism we can begin to understand not only the society in which we as women find ourselves, but the society in which we as young, old, queer, black, disabled, poor, rich, transgender, women, men, workers, parents, activists and students struggle to exist. Intersectional feminism is a lens through which we can define and critique our current struggles, and it is only through intersectionality that feminism can become more inclusive. Through this lens we learn to be sensitive to other people's experiences, we're made aware of how we benefit from systems we didn't make but may perpetuate, and we learn about justice and injustice – not just in reference to women, but in reference to all forms of oppression. In the words of poet Staceyann Chin, 'All oppression is connected.'

I myself have never been able to find out precisely what feminism is: I only know that people call me a feminist whenever I express sentiments that differentiate me from a doormat …

Rebecca West

We live in a culture that wants to put a redemptive face on everything, so anger doesn't sit well with any of us. But I think women's anger sits less well than anything else. Women's anger is very scary to people, and to no one more than to other women, who think my goodness, if I let the lid off, where would we be?

Claire Messud

Sometimes I wonder if men and women really suit each other. Perhaps they should live next door and just visit now and then.

Katharine Hepburn

THIS IS NOT A FEMINIST RANT: THE LANGUAGE OF SILENCING WOMEN

Alice Stride

'You're being very … *animated*,' he said.

We were in a French restaurant, melting raclette and pouring it on potatoes, and I was talking about the pay gap, waving my hands around and sloshing red wine on the table. Indeed, I was being 'very animated' (and perhaps a little pissed). But his words – and tone – stung me, and I fell silent. Not for long, I must say; I'm a near-constant stream of consciousness, universally acknowledged as being an appalling person to watch films with due to my tendency to dissect scenes as they happen – 'The *Titanic* has HIT THE ICEBERG. This indicates that Jack and Rose shall run into some troubles. I can state – with some certainty – that DIFFICULT TIMES ARE AHEAD.'

However, in that moment, I was cowed. It felt as though I wasn't allowed to be 'animated', that I was taking up too much room, too much airtime. The word 'animated' isn't too far removed from 'hysterical' – one of the most gendered words there is. I fell silent and we talked about something else.

Who is this idiot, you ask? How DARE he? Reader, he is not an idiot. He is my wonderful boyfriend: a self-identified feminist who was raised solely by his brilliant mother, a woman who worked long hours as a teacher when he was growing up. He is my biggest cheerleader. He coaches the woman's football team I play in (hi, Tottenham Hotsnatch!) He is not threatened by strong women; he adores them.

So what does it mean if even these great men – the feminist men, with amazing, powerful women in their lives, fully paid-up members of Team Equality – unwittingly shut women down? My boyfriend did not anticipate the way those four little words, coupled with a *slightly* sneering tone, would floor me. And why would he? It was not explicitly misogynistic. He was not deliberately trying to silence me. To repurpose George Michael's classic song, it was a Sexist Whisper – and my guilty feet lost their rhythm.

But, as we live in a patriarchal society, it's to be expected: that even the best guys can unconsciously shut you down, especially when our public figures cannot set an example.

Male leaders continue to turn to the 1950s to startle and silence their female peers.

'Comedian' and television 'star' Daniel O'Reilly (Dapper Laughs) told a woman in the audience at his (somewhat inexplicably) sold-out show at the Scala in October 2014 that she was 'gagging for a rape'. In 2007, Australian politician Bill Hefferman said that Julia Gillard, the country's first female prime minister, had 'no idea what life's about' because she had 'chosen to remain deliberately barren'. (Whilst we're on the subject of language, Mr Hefferman – you didn't need to say 'chosen' AND 'deliberately' in that sentence. You're welcome.)

In June 2015, the Nobel laureate scientist Sir Tim Hunt gave a speech at a conference in South Korea, during which he made comments about his 'trouble with girls' when working with them in the laboratory. It was a feeble attempt at a joke – and it backfired spectacularly on Sir Tim – but even without the media shitstorm that ensued, I am sure some of the 'girls' present at his speech winced.

Our special friends in America fare no better. The radio host Rush Limbaugh dismissed Hillary Clinton as 'just a secretary' (when she was serving as Secretary of State). And, in April 2015, Fox News contributor Erick Erickson delivered some searing insights into Clinton's presidential bid: 'She's going to be old. I don't know how far back they can pull her face.'

These men, this litany of sexist idiots, are threatened. So, they seek to disarm women and shut them up by forcing them to address their femininity (or perceived lack of) and using it against them – a reductive, old-fashioned femininity that they can understand, harking back to a time when women were purely decorative. How do their sexist words make their daughters, friends, wives and sisters feel, I wonder? (I was astounded to discover that some of the seven male MPs who voted ag*ainst* the Equal Pay (Transparency) Bill do indeed have daughters. How do they look them in the eye?)

Male voices are often privileged over female voices. In fact, almost always – which is why, even in 2015, an 'outspoken' woman (i.e. a woman expressing her opinion) is treated like a rare bird. She is sort of fetishised, because she is so unusual. I remember when Lily Allen first burst into the public consciousness – I was seventeen, and I was dizzy with joy. Lily gave her opinion with relish, and she was unafraid to call bullshit – and she was only a few years older than me! My friend did not share my passion for Lily Allen, describing her as 'gobby' and 'too loud'. To my friend, Lily Allen was shocking, and therefore distasteful. Would anyone have referred to the Gallagher brothers as 'gobby' or 'too loud'? Never. Outspoken men are just ... men, living their lives. Outspoken women are 'gobby', or mused over like exotic parrots in a zoo.

I asked my friends for examples of sexist language that has belittled them – in obvious or imperceptible ways. One was told not to get in a 'tizzy' about an email her (male) boss was about to send her. Another told her uncle that she was learning German; he deduced that she was 'looking for a German boyfriend'. Another, after delivering a brilliant presentation to secure a valuable account for the advertising agency she works at was told by her male colleague that she had been a 'good girl' (she is thirty-four). One friend's ex-boyfriend said he was surprised she was doing so well at her job, because 'it's more of a man's job'.

None of them were able to counteract these comments. Responding coherently to sexism can be really bloody hard – so we are left in a perpetual state of WHY DIDN'T I THINK OF THAT HALF AN HOUR AGO WHEN HE SAID THAT TO ME? The moment is gone – but you are still stuck there, flustered and silently raging.

It is a difficult thing to articulate, because language and tone can be so subtle – and it can feel impossible to make the guys understand how entrenched sexism in language is. In fact, I'd wager that the phrase 'It's not *what* you said, it's the *way* you said it' – typically thought of as a 'woman phrase' – IS such because years of patriarchy has made women hyper-aware of the *way* things are said to them. We've had to absorb sexist bullshit like a never-ending lady sponge since the beginning of time; of COURSE we are supremely sensitive to the nuances of it.

Women's Aid, the national domestic violence charity and the organisation that I work for, calls out the sexist behaviour and language that can underpin violence against women and girls. This is because sexist and misogynistic culture devalues and dehumanises women so some men feel it is their right – that they *are entitled* – to abuse. Women's Aid has been working with survivors of domestic violence for forty years, and there is a common thread linking the stories of many of these women: that their abuse started slowly, so slowly that they didn't realise it was happening. Small pieces of their souls were chipped away, bit by bit, often starting with violent, sexist language – 'Silly little woman. You're dumb, do you know that?'

And then, soon, it was normal – the terror, the dark cloud of fear and anxiety that swirled around them – that was normal, and then, suddenly, they were engulfed. The power of psychological abuse, the power of language and its role in the coercive control of women, is not to be underestimated. It is – thankfully – FINALLY being recognised as serious, due to the amazing campaigning work of Women's Aid and others. Section 76 has been introduced into the Serious Crime Act: a new domestic violence law criminalising patterns of coercive, controlling behaviour and psychological abuse. With an average of two women a week being killed at the hands of a partner or ex-partner in England and Wales, Section 76 could not have come a moment too soon.

Of course, I am not claiming that every sexist remark comes from the mouth of an abusive man. That is ridiculous. But we must take a stand against sexist language, no matter how small or inconsequential it may seem at the time.

Why? Because words are the fabric of everything. They can win elections and start wars, and make people fall in love.

Words can save lives and words can save marriages. Words are a comfort and words are a weapon. Words are the heart of life.

We must be empowered to call out the sexist whispers that make us lose our rhythm – even when it's coming from the mouths of our brothers, our friends, our partners, our fathers. And this problem goes all the way to the top – so we need to start at the bottom. If we do not address sexist language, we will not drive the change we need to stop women being viewed as second-class citizens. The change needed to stop some men believing it is their fucking *right* to intimidate women. The change we need to stop some men believing that a woman's life is over because he has decided so.

I had a conversation with a close male relative about feminism: why it is vital, and why I maintain my right to be furious about sexism and inequality, to keep pushing for a better world. He insisted that as things are 'better for women than they used to be' there was nothing to be fighting against any more.

'The problem with *you feminists*,' he said, 'is that nowadays I feel like I can't say ANYTHING – even if it's a *joke*. You just get *hysterical* about everything.'

And there – in one fell, sexist swoop – he proved my point. Thanks for that, *dear*.

I do not wish [women] to have power over men; but over themselves.

Mary Wollstonecraft, A Vindication of the Rights of Woman

Feminism isn't about making women stronger. Women are already strong. It's about changing the way the world perceives that strength.

G. D. Anderson

It's called *Yes Please* because it is the constant struggle and often the right answer. Can we figure out what we want, ask for it, and stop talking? Yes please. Is being vulnerable a power position? Yes please. Am I allowed to take up space? Yes please. Would you like to be left alone? Yes please.

Amy Poehler, Yes Please

I CALL MYSELF A FEMINIST

June Eric-Udorie

I didn't always call myself a feminist. I swore the word would never cross my lips. Feminism came with too much baggage. I never heard anything positive about feminists, and I vividly remember my mother warning me in hushed tones that feminists were jealous women, upset that they had failed to get husbands. I was told that feminists wanted to kill all men, that they burned their bras and were lesbians. When I asked my teacher about what I now know is sexism, I was reminded that 'good girls who were brought up properly by a Christian mother' did not ask such questions. I vowed to never be a feminist and I rejected the label. I stopped asking too many questions and I stopped talking 'too much', and family and friends congratulated me because men didn't like women who talked too much.

But the older I got, the more I found myself fighting the urge to speak, to question, to shout and to take up space. I sat on my hands and bit my tongue, but it didn't last long. I was angry about the sexism I saw on a daily basis. I wanted to speak up about it, to ask why my mother said whistling was for boys, to question why the boys were always the ones assumed to be good at maths, and to talk at the top of my tiny lungs when my mother told me to keep quiet because 'good girls were supposed to be seen not heard'. I *had* to question the problem with gender around me, so at eleven, I thought, 'Fuck it, I'm going to call myself a feminist.'

Growing up in Nigeria, I was surrounded by institutionalised sexism and misogyny. Women experiencing domestic violence in their marriage were told they were 'lucky' to have husbands. At dinner parties, people joked that my mother only 'gave' my father three daughters and encouraged her to try her luck to see if she might have a son. I heard horror stories of women who had been raped and who killed themselves. I watched in disbelief as the little girls living in my neighbourhood were married aged nine or ten to men old enough to be their fathers, and in some cases their grandfathers.

The eleven-year-old me was desperate to do something and calling myself a feminist seemed like the first step, but equally a dangerous step. But I did it. I called myself a feminist. I didn't *become* one, because I already believed in and was eager for gender equality. Calling myself a feminist was standing up to say that women are people and they deserve liberation. Calling myself a feminist was breaking away from the silence, was not being complicit, and was the first step I took to acknowledging that I would join the fight for women's liberation. I soon realised that oppression, misogyny and violence against women were vicious plagues. I saw sexism everywhere and in everything. It was too much for the eleven-year-old me and I became exhausted and frustrated that the issue was so omnipresent and yet so neglected.

I also saw how prevalent it was in one of my favourite places, the Church.

I grew up in a very religious family and it never crossed my mind that Christianity, and religion in general, could contribute to the oppression of women and the denial of our fundamental human rights. It was and remains the only place I find it difficult to call out sexism and misogyny. I sat angrily when the pastor preached that men should pick the names for their children because women are 'irrational and emotional'. I was angry but I said nothing when he banned short skirts and joked that 'an usher might come and complete your dressing'.

It was hard for me to fight the urge to speak in church and I didn't always manage to keep quiet. A discussion on abortion began and I found myself saying that I believed in abortion on demand. I knew that it was the 'wrong' thing to do in a room full of people who were pro-life, but I felt proud that I had done so. Having been pro-life myself, to publicly acknowledge that I was no longer pro-life but now pro-choice felt like a big step forward. I was pulled to the side, told in hushed tones that I had to stop thinking I was a 'white person' and remember where I came from. I was reminded that this 'feminism' that had corrupted me was not part of my culture, it was incompatible with my religion and it was un-African.

Being a feminist is hard. Being somewhat religious and being a feminist has felt, at times, unbearable. I have fought with my mother on innumerable occasions, about everything from the notion that women must be 'submissive' to men, to why a woman should have full bodily autonomy. I have felt conflicted many times: do I have to drop Christianity to be a 'true' feminist? It is not a question I have an answer to, and I suspect I never will. What makes feminism special, I think, is that there are no definite answers to tough questions; we must come up with the answers ourselves in this radical movement for change.

I watch too many girls turn their noses up at feminism. I watch too many girls lose their confidence when they hit puberty. I watch too many girls limit themselves because they don't want to be called 'ambitious' or 'bossy'. I am a teenage girl – I have been there too. I have worried, endlessly, about other people's perceptions of me. I wanted to be liked – who didn't?

I am a feminist because I want to be rebellious. Girls and women are always expected to be the silent watchers in society and *always* to be well behaved. I think that's nonsense and I wish all women would see that too. I wish more girls and women would give likability the middle finger. I wish more girls could see their potential to shake the world. I wish more girls and women could see the double standards and the perpetual state of wrongness, and no longer care what other people think.

I wish more girls and women could learn that the most revolutionary act they can make is to be their brilliant selves.

As a teenager, feminism appealed to me because I knew I deserved to be free and I was willing to fight and rebel to achieve that. At nearly seventeen, I feel like my rebellion has only just started. I am always disobedient; the stereotypes and rules that are forced onto girls are things I actively try to break away from even if I know it will get me into trouble. Because as we have learned from Laurel Thatcher Ulrich, 'well-behaved women seldom make history'.

It may sound clichéd, but feminism saved me. I didn't have a choice; it was either become a feminist or go crazy. It gave me the ability to do many things that were inconceivable to me a few years ago. I no longer feel intimidated by men and I will never put myself down to impress a man. I found freedom from the societal expectations of what it meant to be a 'woman' because I was surrounded by women who defied every notion within that. I found a space where I learned that I was not alone, and I found solidarity and love.

Most of all, feminism gave me the permission to be.

Women and girls are so often not given the permission to be. We are told what it means to be us. We are instructed, given a set of rules that we must follow, and when we don't the consequences are insurmountable. We are put into small boxes and squashed, because allowing a woman to be herself is a threat to those who want to continue to have the power in society. We are constantly worried that if we cannot fulfil the impossible expectations placed on us, we have failed. And to that, I say: *bullshit.* I want every girl to have the permission to be human. Feminism gave me that, the permission to be me: to be loud, to cry, to speak, to dance like nobody is watching, to protest, to support, to sing at the top of my voice, to love and to question.

The journalist and author Mona Eltahawy asked the girls of the Middle East and North Africa to 'be immodest, rebel, disobey and know you deserve to be free'. This has become my mantra. I want *all* girls and women to be immodest, disobedient rebels because the only way to win the battle for our liberation is if we collectively break away from the profound shitness of the expectations of 'womanhood' in our world.

I call myself a feminist. I am a feminist. And nothing is ever going to change that.

When I was in college, a teacher once said that all women live by a 'rape schedule'. I was baffled by the term, but as she went on to explain, I got really freaked out. Because I realized that I knew exactly what she was talking about. And you do too. Because of their constant fear of rape (conscious or not), women do things throughout the day to protect themselves. Whether it's carrying our keys in our hands as we walk home, locking our car doors as soon as we get in, or not walking down certain streets, we take precautions. While taking precautions is certainly not a bad idea, the fact that certain things women do are so ingrained into our daily routines is truly disturbing. It's essentially like living in a prison – all the time. We can't assume that we're safe anywhere: not on the streets, not in our homes. And we're so used to feeling unsafe that we don't even see that there's something seriously fucked up about it.

Jessica Valenti, Full Frontal Feminism

Within days of winning the Foster's award [in 2013], journalists were already asking 'so what's next?', as if I'd said all there was to say on the subject [of feminism]. Or that I'd fixed everything. Yes, all the misogynists came, loved it and have stopped with all the oppressing now. Didn't I do well? No, I didn't. If anything, I've made things worse. I wondered whether male comics were asked the same thing. 'So, Robin Ince, you've been angry for quite a few years now, about various things, like God and badly written books, don't you think it's time you moved on to something else now? What about doing some mime, Robin? Or learning the ukulele and singing some songs about sweets, ghosts or mud?' And Andy Zaltzman. Andy Zaltzman must have done politics by now?! Surely it's time he moved on to the ecosystem or DIY or cats?

When a female comic talks passionately about issues, she is 'whingeing' or 'moaning', but a male comic doing the same thing is principled, committed and passionate. Mark Thomas, for example, didn't 'bleat on' about the arms trade, did he? He spoke powerfully, bravely and emotionally about an issue that was important to him. I look forward to a time when a woman's voice, publicly expressing an opinion, isn't compared to that of a sheep or a goat. I don't know what I'll be doing in five or ten years' time, I'll probably be dead, but for now, there's still plenty to be 'banging on' about. To quote Helen Lewis, the journalist, 'the comments on any article about feminism justify feminism'.

Bridget Christie

... I think the first real change in women's body image came when JLo turned it butt-style. That was the first time that having a large-scale situation in the back was part of *mainstream* American beauty. Girls wanted butts now. Men were free to admit that they had always enjoyed them. And then, what felt like *moments* later, boom – Beyoncé brought the leg meat. A back porch and thick muscular legs were now widely admired. And from that day forward, women embraced their diversity and realized that all shapes and sizes are beautiful. Ah ha ha. No. I'm totally messing with you. All Beyoncé and JLo have done is add to the laundry list of attributes women must have to qualify as beautiful. Now every girl is expected to have:

- Caucasian blue eyes
- full Spanish lips
- a classic button nose
- hairless Asian skin with a California tan
- a Jamaican dance hall ass
- long Swedish legs
- small Japanese feet
- the abs of a lesbian gym owner

- the hips of a nine-year-old boy
- the arms of Michelle Obama
- and doll tits

The person closest to actually achieving this look is Kim Kardashian, who, as we know, was made by Russian scientists to sabotage our athletes.

Tina Fey, Bossypants

There is no female mind. The brain is not an organ of sex. As well speak of a female liver.

Charlotte Perkins Gilman, Women and Economics

TALKING ABOUT MY GENERATION

Tania Shew

I am not often proud of my generation. It sometimes seems like we are immersed in a culture of materialism and individualism. Rather than 'Revolution', 'We Shall Overcome' or 'I Am Woman', we produce songs entitled 'Millionaire', 'Waking Up In Vegas' and 'Fancy'. We consume TV shows filled with beautiful people living in beautiful houses, owning beautiful possessions and not doing very much else. As a history student I have studied the French revolutionaries, the Suffragettes, Rosa Parks and the Ford Dagenham workers and I often think, why can't we be more like them? Why can't we be less self-serving? Why can't we be more concerned about the moral examples we will leave our children than the accumulations of wealth we'll write in our wills? But in feminism, I see the more selfless side of my generation. I see groups of people trying to be the best they can be and, for the most part, trying to make the world a better place for everyone. Being part of these groups inspires me to try to be better. I have already been on a bit of a journey, and I have certainly made mistakes, but that's why I call myself a feminist.

I am very fortunate to have grown up in a feminist household. From the time I could toddle my mum started reading me children's adaptations of the lives of the Pankhursts and relayed stories of her times in women's groups in the 1970s and '80s. I was weaned on this vague mix of first- and second-wave values, but it wasn't until I was sixteen that I realised a new wave was emerging and that I could be a part of it. Not long after I started sixth form at the Camden School for Girls (founded by a Suffragist in 1871 as one of the first girls' schools to cater for young women of all backgrounds), I discovered a student in the year above was founding a feminist group, and I joined as one of its first members. Here, during weekly discussions about catcalling, slut-shaming and casual sexist language, I tentatively began to fully comprehend that feminism could encompass so much more than legal rights and formal equality, and came to recognise sexism in all its forms, whenever I encountered it.

Our first campaign as a group was to combat the displaying of 'lads' mags' at eye-level in the branch of Tesco across the road from our school, which most of the pupils frequented to buy their lunches. After reading an article which demonstrated that sometimes it can be difficult to distinguish the text in top 'lads'" publications from quotes by convicted rapists, we became concerned about these magazines intruding on the lunch breaks of hundreds of young girls; we were anxious about this resulting in a potential increase in body-confidence issues and girls growing up unconsciously absorbing the message that they need to objectify themselves to attract male attention. As feminists, we too were uncomfortable with these portrayals of women impacting on our everyday lives, and so began our mission to get the magazines displayed on a higher shelf or have the front-cover images covered up. We started by talking to staff at the branch and then made a short film (or docufemtry, as we called it) demonstrating how students, teachers and customers shared a concern at the way these images were being displayed. After months of campaigning we eventually won, with the magazines being removed from the store entirely. This campaign led our group to morph from a small, unknown school club to one receiving attention from the national press.

During my time with the Camden School for Girls fem club I got my first glimpses of the feminist world. We received lessons in how to run campaigns, we raised hundreds of pounds for women's charities and we also learned, from experience, some of the challenges of operating in a feminist space. In our co-educational sixth form we of course wanted our group to be open to students of all genders, but we soon encountered some of the challenges that could accompany this. The few male members often dominated the conversations and were sometimes given a more prominent position in photo shoots.

I was personally very fortunate in that membership of this group gave me the opportunity to meet a number of inspirational feminists, such as Kat Banyard and Charlotte Raven, which led to my being asked to join an advisory group for UK Feminista by the former and the editorial board of *Feminist Times* by the latter.

Needless to say, by the time I started university as a slightly precocious eighteen-year-old, I felt I had a fair amount of experience of feminism. Yet I couldn't have been more wrong. I had learned to run before I could walk and still had a long way to go. My first shock was how sheltered I had been from sexism. Growing up in the left-wing, *Guardian*-reading bubble that is Kentish Town, it turned out I actually had no idea how much misogyny goes unnoticed and unchallenged in many circles. On one of my first nights at uni I struck up a conversation with a guy at the campus bar. The moment I mentioned I'd been to an all-girls school he deduced that I must be a 'slut'. When I questioned his use of the term, and indeed the very concept of female promiscuity being an innately negative thing, he defended himself with the 'good key, bad lock' analogy. The shock of these completely casual sexist remarks and beliefs, made right to my face, struck me forcibly and made me realise how relatively protected I'd been so far. I soon learned that many young men have no problem making rape jokes or singing misogynistic chants. I also discovered how many people of all genders are turned off by the word 'feminism' or do not think it is relevant to them. When fundraising for my university femsoc last Christmas, I approached some male members of the Christian Society standing at a stall near by and told them I'd take one of their flyers if they came along to a meeting. The two boys looked at me, perplexed, and announced they couldn't come to a feminist meeting because they were men.

At university I also discovered how misguided I had previously been in my feminism. In sixth form I had enjoyed spending one hour a week feeling unadulteratedly righteous and united against the common enemy of sexual prejudice. But at university I realised that I could be part of the problem too. I learned that whilst I am entitled to be angry about the sexism I experience, many people have worse experiences of sexism than me, or experiences of sexism that intersect with other forms of prejudice or hatred such as racism, homophobia, classism or trans-misogyny. I learned to move away from the 'Patricia Arquette school of feminism' (one guided by the interests of the white middle classes) and broaden my horizons. I realised that behind modern feminism there is a core impetus for 'doing the right thing' in all manner of situations. Many of the feminists I know try to be principled in their actions, words and values in an attempt not just to end the forms of sexism that they experience themselves, but, rather ambitiously, to bring down the whole kyriarchy. Whilst, contrary to stereotypes, all the feminists I met at university were up for a good laugh, this was never to come at the expense of their core ethics. Feminism, therefore, is a movement I strongly believe in. Sitting in our cosy meeting places, gorging on custard creams, I feel that fiery sprit I've read about in so many history books. I see groups of young people all determined to make the world a better place. I see a generation I can be proud of.

If we value what we've inherited for free – from other women – surely it's right morally and ethically for us to wake up and say, 'I'm a feminist …'

Annie Lennox

I'm a feminist. I've been a female for a long time now. It'd be stupid not to be on my own side.

Maya Angelou

'Why do men feel threatened by women?' I asked a male friend of mine.

'They are afraid women will laugh at them,' he said, 'undercut their world view.'

Then I asked some women students, 'Why do women feel threatened by men?'

'They are afraid of being killed,' they said.

Margaret Atwood

‘ROTI KAMANA’: STORIES OF SURVIVAL

Samira Shackle

From the outside, the house is unremarkable. Situated in an up-and-coming district of Islamabad, the surrounding streets are dominated by construction, with apartment blocks springing up to accommodate the city’s gradually expanding population.

It is a large house, but not distinct from any of the others on the street, which are all generously sized and set back from the road. I ring the bell, and am greeted by an employee, who hands me two small plastic pouches, of the type you might find at a swimming pool to cover your shoes. ‘We can’t let any dirt get in,’ says the man at the door, apologetically. I cover my feet with the bags and walk in.

The Acid Survivors’ Foundation (ASF) is the only centre

in Pakistan dedicated to the treatment and rehabilitation of victims of acid violence. The centre provides accommodation for victims while they receive medical, legal and psychological support. It also provides a space for victims to meet other women – and it tends to be women – in the same situation as themselves.

Acid violence is exactly what the name suggests: it involves a corrosive substance, usually sulphuric acid, being thrown at a victim. It takes seconds to carry out an attack, but can cause permanent disability, as well as disfigurement and excruciating pain. Skin melts, muscles fuse together, vision is lost. If the wounds are not immediately flushed with clean water, the injuries are compounded. It is an astonishingly brutal crime that strikes at the very identity of the victim.

Fortunately, acid crimes are not hugely widespread. According to the international organisation the Acid Survivors Trust, around 1500 cases are recorded worldwide every year, with about 150 of those in Pakistan. But its extremity makes it notable, and as the crime is under-reported the real figures are likely to be far higher. There are no hard and fast rules – men can be victims and women can be perpetrators. But for the most part, it tends to be a form of gender-based violence. As such, it is more prevalent in countries where women are disenfranchised: not just Pakistan, but also India, Nepal, Bangladesh, Colombia, Vietnam and Cambodia. In Pakistan and elsewhere in south Asia, the crime is made easy by the ready availability of acid, which is used in the cotton industry to treat the seeds and clean the fibres. It is also used as a cheap cleaning fluid for machinery and in the home. A bottle of acid costs around twenty pence.

The ASF house in Islamabad is permeated by a faint smell of disinfectant. The surgical procedures to repair the damage from acid attacks can take months, involving skin grafts and other operations, so it's important that those convalescing here are not exposed to infection.

This is something that Zainab knows all about. An articulate girl of seventeen, she tells me that she has lost count of how many operations she has had. Her grafted skin is shiny and uneven in colour, in places crinkled like crêpe paper. She is permanently blind in one eye, which is frozen open as a result of the attack. The image of her former self is present in the corner of her face that was untouched by the acid: her right eye and its long lashes, the prominent cheekbone below. For years after the attack, she says, she would only leave the house wearing a headscarf that covered all of her face, apart from this section. She wraps her scarf around her face to show me, covering up the false eye, the patchwork of skin grafts.

'It felt like someone had put fire on me,' she tells me, her hand running over a mini foosball table that has recently been bought to keep survivors entertained. 'No one could forget that pain. It stays all your life.'

The most striking aspect of Zainab's case is the triviality of the attacker's motives. The neighbour's son had proposed to Zainab's sister. She didn't want to marry him, and said no. A few weeks later, he broke into their house at night to exact revenge, armed with a bottle of acid. He got the wrong sister. Zainab was twelve years old.

The other women at the ASF refuge have similar tales to tell: men taking revenge for rejected marriage proposals, husbands who got bored with their wives. Their lives were destroyed in an instant, for no discernible reason. Mohammad Jawad, a plastic surgeon who appeared in *Saving Face*, the documentary about acid attacks in Pakistan that won an Oscar in 2012, has described it thus: 'The attacker is saying: "I don't want to kill her – I am going to do something to distort her." It's a walking-dead situation for the victim.'

After years of medical and psychological support, Zainab is starting to see some hope in the future. She speaks in a monotone while she recounts the details of the attack and her family's failed attempts to get justice, but lights up when she says she has learned to read. 'I want to go out there and step into the world and experience life like I deserve to.' She glows with pride describing how she recently travelled to Bangladesh to address a conference on acid crimes.

Yet the small humiliations are still hard to bear. She describes going to a government office to register for an ID card. The woman behind the desk asked, pointedly,

'What happened to your face?' As she relates this story, Zainab begins to cry. 'Why can't people let me live my life normally?'

When I leave ASF, I feel dizzy, overwhelmed by the suffering of these women, their powerlessness. It is hard to tell where misogyny ends and class oppression begins. Mostly coming from impoverished areas, these women had very little to begin with in terms of rights, opportunity or money, and now the very fabric of their being has been attacked too. Acid crimes tend to happen in conservative regions where women are severely constrained. Some of the women I met were still living with their attacker, which they saw as preferable to enduring the second stigma of being a divorced woman. Some were illiterate, and had been deceived into signing statements absolving their assailants. Transcribing their interviews the next day in the comfort of my flat in Islamabad, I weep, aware that my response is unhelpful.

But as I transcribe, I begin to notice some glimmers of hope. One woman had lost the use of her arm as well as one of her eyes. Over the course of months of painful surgeries and physiotherapy, she slowly regained the use of the arm. That, for her, was the psychological turning point. She was able to make bread again, which meant that she knew she could provide for herself and for her children. The Urdu phrase 'roti kamana', to earn one's daily bread, ties together self-sufficiency and nourishment. For anyone else, the triumph of making roti again might seem insignificant, but for this woman it meant sustenance, independence and femininity, in the most powerful sense of the word.

It is the parting sentiment of Saida, a woman who had been attacked by a bored husband, that stays with me. 'Initially, I used to cry and I used to scream, but now, truly in my heart, I don't think I'm ugly,' she said. 'I feel that I'm beautiful and I don't think I have anything to fear.'

Acid-throwing is a crime aimed at erasing identity, a particularly extreme form of gender violence. In keeping their sense of self intact, these women are committing a profound act of defiance.

… the most contemptible of all lives is where you live in the world, and none of your passions or affections are brought into action. I am convinced I could not live thus …

Mary Shelley

your thorns are the best part of you.

Marianne Moore, 'Roses Only'

… it's also rare, and I'm not sure why, to find women who combine humour and opinion. I think it's impressed on women, early on, that holding forth politically is an unattractive trait. One of the few ways for women to make a mark is to do what I've done and take over a show. It changes the tone. As soon as my boys come out for our recording I make them all kiss me. Immediately we've established a more nurturing atmosphere.

Sandi Toksvig

Types of Women in Romantic Comedies Who Are Not Real

The Skinny Woman Who is Beautiful and Toned but also Gluttonous and Disgusting

[I] am more than willing to suspend my disbelief during a romantic comedy …

But sometimes even my suspended disbelief isn't enough. I am speaking of the gorgeous and skinny heroine who is also a disgusting pig when it comes to food. And everyone in the movie – her parents, her friends, her boss – are all complicit in this huge lie. They are constantly telling her to stop eating and being such a glutton. And this actress, this poor skinny actress who so clearly lost weight to play the likeable lead, has to say things like 'Shut up you guys! I love cheesecake! If I want to eat an entire cheesecake, I will!' If you look closely, you can see this woman's ribs through the dress she's wearing – that's how skinny she is, this cheesecake-loving cow.

You wonder, as you sit and watch this movie, what the characters would do if they were confronted by an actual average American woman. They would all kill themselves, which would actually be kind of an interesting movie.

Mindy Kaling, Is Everyone Hanging Out with Me?

I CALL MYSELF A FEMINIST WITH MY ELBOWS

Amy Annette

[A short stand-up monologue to be read out loud and proud (or in your head)]

Hello there! How's everyone doing tonight? Hey, before I really get into it and talk about how important it is to take up space in this world as a woman, before I let you know how, just by existing, you make powerful statements of courage every day, and before I note that that's all happening with or without you consciously living a life steered by feminism – I've just got a quick question to ask the ladies in the house. Don't worry, this isn't an audience participation bit – I'm sure you'll know the answer to this one.

'What does your body say about you?'

Now, if you're confused or don't understand the question that may be because the question is actually written in a unique modern language called 'Women's Magazinese'. I'm sure most of you have at least a basic understanding of it even if you don't speak it. It's a language you mostly read, anyway … like the ancient languages of Latin, Greek or Wingdings. And of course there are offshoot dialects of Women's Magazinese such as the 'Language of Fruits' – but don't worry, I'm not asking you to identify yourself as a Pear, Apple or Potato in body shape or in spirit.

But actually, in this instance, and looked at from another perspective, I think we should answer this question honestly: 'What does my body say about me?'

Not in a reductive 'what-does-your-choice-of-sock-colour-indicate-about-how-good-a-mother-you'll-be' magazine-article kind of way, but more in a do-you-realise-how-political-your-body-and-the-space-it-inhabits-is? kind of way, that recognises just how much you're saying to the world when, to quote the great Ronan Keating, 'you say nothing at all …'

I call myself a feminist with my body.

So much of communication is non-verbal – we proclaim

our self-confidence as we pound down the street with a straight back, unashamed, filling the world with our vibrancy, unafraid to be visible. We try to hide our vulnerability when we hunch our way past a group of loud drunks. 'You can't talk to me! I'm all shoulders and we all know shoulders don't have ears!'

Sometimes we consciously position ourselves. A trick I have, that I've never said out loud before this – and in writing it out I perhaps realise it's foolishness but will nevertheless continue to use it, I'm sure – is to rub my jaw as if I'm in great pain whenever I'm out and about and uncomfortable in a situation. I think my logic is that only the very, very, VERY worst of humans would mess with someone with toothache. I'm removing myself from greater conflict by showing them how deep my own conflict is; see also long fringes covering eyes, deeply lined kohl-black eyes and Green Day iron-on badges (hey, listen, I grew up in the late nineties/early noughties).

What an amazing amount of information to convey without speaking. We say a lot without opening our mouths. Not wearing make-up? You're a natural beauty, or perhaps you're raising cash for charity. Wearing six-inch heels? You're a victim of the patriarchy's obsession with weak ankles, or you're in charge of your own sexuality and style. Body hair on display? You're a statement-maker whose phone autocorrects 'history' to 'herstory', or you hate the feeling of leg fuzz and you're on your way to having it waxed off and have let it grow to exactly the right mm length to minimise pain.

Wearing a full clown suit with requisite face paint? You're a clown, or you want to be a clown (live your dreams).

I call myself a feminist with my elbows.

Sometimes owning your own space means protecting your own unique identity from assimilation; sometimes it's entering feet-first into tradition and not being cowed by it; sometimes it's not letting someone overlook you for a job or opportunity because of your gender; and sometimes it's just about refusing to be stepped on on your way to work. Eight a.m. on my commute, when I'm spending much of my journey trying to protect my toes from the hard leather of a smart shoe, is when I feel the frustration of literally having to fight for my own space in the world. I send out a battle cry from my elbow of 'NO THANK YOU, SIR' as it sticks into the soft underarm seam of blue-striped suit to protect my face from armpit-to-nostril contact. I will stand up for myself when necessary, even though I'd always much rather just have a seat on the Tube, and take my allotted space as a woman and fare-payer, evading the evil of 'manspreading' which makes it impossible to sit down without gaining an intimate knowledge of the knee grooves of your neighbour.

It's not just the toe-steppers. My space is encroached upon in many ways as I hurtle beneath the city. I say 'NOT FOR ME, CHEERS' with my eyes when subjected to another 'Beach Body Ready' article or advertisement and then I watch the eyes of the women next to me also taking it in and I revise it to 'NOT FOR US, THANKS'. I want to get to work without having to feel aggressed, sad for all women ever and – frankly the worst of all modern sins – badly marketed to.

I live in London, so forgive me if the references to dealing with people at close quarters on public transport don't chime with you, but day to day it continues to be a great example of how your body, even sitting down and inert, with bags hanging from every limb, can be political. Refusing someone the entirety of the shared armrest by letting your arm rest where it naturally should – even if that means using their arm as a sort of flesh pillow for your shoulder – it's honestly so radical! You are taking your space without embarrassment that you'll be considered unladylike or thought too large for the space. And even if they do think that of you, or even say that to you, that's still infinitely better than spending your commute in a sweaty embrace of yourself, arms clasped closely across your heart just to fit into the space allowed to you.

I call myself a feminist with my hair.

Some aspects of the female body should be allowed a second vote at election time they are so uniquely politicised. You might think: sure, my body hair is long but it's not yet so thick as to actually take up space; but have you ever sat on the bus and had two tourists point and laugh at your body hair in a language you don't understand, somehow making it worse? To be honest, NO, I haven't – that happened to my friend Sas – and that wasn't even in the period when she was dying her armpit hair blue. You are engaging in a major statement with any kind of body hair and currently there's nothing quite so loud as the unchecked growth of hair under your arms or between or on your legs. But there's also a space for hair removal and feminism. Hair and your own identity as a woman and a feminist is already so widely talked about that you feel like you're dialling in to a worldwide feminist conference call every time you pluck a hair – **pluck** the Suffragettes **pluck** Susan Sontag **pluck** Tina Fey **pluck**. Surely there are more important things to be thinking about than my imminent monobrow? **pluck** Kim Kardashian ...

I call myself a feminist with my big butt.

I think women over a certain size – I won't say a number here because it's meaningless, reductive and frankly illogical to say 'size 12: Well Done', 'size 14: Could Try Harder' and then suddenly jump to 'size 16: BAD! BAD! BAD!' when everyone knows women who don't fit these numbers and happily exist with a size 20 top half, a size 16 middle half, and a size 8 bottom half (we women are mysterious many-halfed creatures) – I think women over a certain size live life more consciously aware of space. That's because we (oops, just outed myself there as a 'BAD! BAD! BAD!') take up more of it just by existing.

I know of what I speak when I talk about the politics of taking up space, because it's with me at all times. Every time I go to sit down at a restaurant table I have to think, is my bum going to send the condiments flying? You may not set out thinking yourself a warrior of women every time you negotiate the tables at Nando's, but you are every time you firmly press into a crowded place or wear clothes other than those that 'flatter' you by erecting tent-like structures over your lumps and bumps. That spray of Peri-Peri salt across the floor is a tiny tickertape parade for you and your butt.

I call myself a feminist with my stride.

I'm conscious of how much space I'm taking up most of the time. Sometimes I feel like I'm too big for the space and sometimes I feel like I deserve more. Both feelings fill me with a desire for action and an important platform for this personal action is on the street. I try to get from one end of a road to the other without allowing anyone – honestly, mostly men – to force me to move out of their way. Once you're conscious of how often you swivel and twist you can't go back to that. Part of my wake-up call was an article I read online in *New York Magazine* (the city that can probably best lay claim to being the home of the aggressive male stride) which came about through one woman's decision to not move out of the way and see how many men and women would smack into her or make her fall. Next time you walk down a busy street see how many times you have to move out of the way or risk a collision. I thought about how, even with my privilege of being able-bodied, I find it hard, and I thought of the flinches and shoulder shrugs I do to slip past the crowd – how I dance through the streets of London every day – and I redoubled my efforts to take up as much space as I safely could, whenever I could.

I call myself a feminist with my heart ...

The true summation, however schlocky, of this short monologue that you can read out to your nearest and dearest, your fellow commuters, or just to yourself on the loo is: I just want more women to know how brilliant they are – every time – when they walk down a street and refuse to duck and dive, when they're not cowed into toning down their vibrancy outside to avoid notice, when they wax their pubic hair into their star sign or simply refuse to be ignored either by leaning in or just plain elbowing their way in as they wish. I'd like more women to simply be conscious of what space they aren't given easily, don't take or could be taking. Space isn't the final frontier – it's the frontier that we fight on every day. I'm proud of you.

[*Long pause here whilst looking deeply into the eye of every woman in your audience until it gets uncomfortable to really increase the effect of the sincerity; and refuse to leave the stage until everyone is giving you a standing* O.]

A dame that knows the ropes isn't likely to get tied up.

Mae West

It is in vain to say human beings ought to be satisfied with tranquillity; they must have action; and they will make it if they cannot find it. Millions are condemned to a stiller doom than mine, and millions are in silent revolt against their lot. Nobody knows how many rebellions, besides political rebellions, ferment in the masses of life which people earth. Women are supposed to be very calm generally; but women feel just as men feel; they need exercise for their faculties, and a field for their efforts, as much as their brothers do; they suffer from too rigid a restraint, too absolute a stagnation, precisely as men would suffer; and it is narrow-minded in their more privileged fellow-creatures to say that they ought to confine themselves to making puddings and knitting stockings, to playing on the piano and embroidering bags. It is thoughtless to condemn them, or laugh at them, if they seek to do more or learn more than custom has pronounced necessary for their sex.

Charlotte Brontë, Jane Eyre

So is there anything intrinsically wrong with the fact that 25 per cent of employed Yale graduates end up in [the consulting and finance] industry?

Yeah. I think so.

Of course this is my own opinion, but to me there's something sad about so many of us entering a line of work in which we're not (for the most part) producing something, or helping someone, or engaging in something that we're explicitly passionate about. Even if it's just for two or three years. That's a lot of years! And these aren't just years. This is twenty-three and twenty-four and twenty-five. If it were a smaller percentage of people, perhaps it wouldn't bother me so much. But it's not.

What it boils down to is that we could be doing other things. Sure, working at Bain or McKinsey or J.P. Morgan might be one way to gain skills to help us get hired elsewhere, but it's obviously not the only option. There's a lot of cool shit we could all be doing – and I don't need to enumerate the clichés.

Obviously, some people need to make money. They have school loans to pay off and families to support. For those of us with an actual need to make money quickly, these industries might make a lot of sense. In fact, I think that working hard to earn a decent amount of money can be quite noble. I'm still struggling with the fact that due to my own (selfish) desire to be a writer, my children probably won't have the same opportunities I had growing up. For most students, however, I genuinely don't think it's about the money. It's a factor, sure. But it just feels like a factor.

What bothers me is this idea of validation, of rationalization. The notion that some of us (regardless of what we tell ourselves) are doing this because we're not sure what else to do and it's easy to apply to and it will pay us decently and it will make us feel like we're still successful. I just haven't met that many people who sound genuinely excited about these jobs. That's super depressing! I don't understand why no one is talking about it.

Oftentimes at Yale, I'll be sitting around studying or drinking or hanging out when I'll hear one of my friends talk about a project they're doing for a class or a rally they're organizing or a play they're putting on. And I'll just think, really, honestly, how remarkably privileged we are to hang around with such a talented group of people around here. I am constantly reminded of the immense passion and creativity of those with whom I get to spend time every day.

Maybe I am overreacting. Maybe it really is a fantastic way to gain valuable, real-world skills. And maybe everyone will quit these jobs in a few years and do something else.

But it worries me.

I want to watch [my friend] Shloe's movies and I want to see Mark's musicals and I want to volunteer with Joe's nonprofit and eat at Annie's restaurant and send my kids to schools Jeff has reformed and I'm *just scared* about this industry that's taking all my friends and telling them this is the best way for them to be spending their time. Any of their time. Maybe I'm ignorant and idealistic but I just feel like that can't possibly be true. I feel like we know that. I feel like we can do something really cool to this world. And I fear – at twenty-three, twenty-four, twenty-five – we might forget.

Marina Keegan, The Opposite of Loneliness

Look to yourself. You free. Nothing and nobody is obliged to save you but you. Seed your own land. You young and a woman and there's serious limitation in both, but you a person too ... Somewhere inside you is that free person I'm talking about. Locate her and let her do some good in the world.

Toni Morrison, Home

… people laugh at me because I use big words. But if you have big ideas you have to use big words to express them, haven't you?

L. M. Montgomery, Anne of Green Gables

A TYPICAL ENGINEER

Naomi Mitchison

The Typical Engineer gets really, really excited by things not working. If they are behaving in a new and unpredictable way he's never seen before, so much the better. One time my lab partner and I accidentally broke a circuit. We gave it to the lecturer, who took it away to 'have a look'. We had evidently broken it in a very interesting way because the lecturer spent the next few weeks emailing us, often well into the night, with updates on which bits he had taken apart, what bugs he had spotted along the way, and how he was going to fix them. Eventually, he got so engrossed in fixing one particular issue that it distracted him entirely from the original fault (and probably from the day job too). When we graduated the following year, we were still receiving his enthusiastic updates.

The Typical Engineer loves having toys to play with. He loves nothing more than to be given some useful bits of equipment (ideally dating from the early nineties) and an object that is either broken (as above) or designed by someone else and therefore has 'scope for improvement'. He then wants to be left alone for days or weeks to potter around and make something that is clever, intricate and beautiful – if entirely unusable.

The Typical Engineer refuses, on principle, to read user manuals.

The Typical Engineer has strong opinions about obscure technical details that the rest of the world doesn't understand (and doesn't even want to understand) such as whether a counting system should start at 1 or 0, or whether the square root of minus 1 should be called 'i' or 'j'.

The Typical Engineer has dedicated shed space set aside for engineering projects that are deemed too unsafe to carry out at work. These often involve lathes, nail guns and circular saws.

The Typical Engineer is a hoarder: he never wants to throw away that broken bit of circuit or that snippet of green wire 'just in case it comes in handy some time'. Never mind that no one knows what it is or what it does. Never mind that he can't see his desk for the piles of junk. Never mind that technological progress now means an identical component can be ordered online for twenty-five pence and delivered to his desk the following day.

The Typical Engineer enjoys arguing. He likes a good robust discussion, and enjoys being challenged. While respecting solid evidence and strong arguments, he will often continue to defend his point just for fun. Of course he assumes the same is true of everyone else …

The Typical Engineer absorbs obscure information, which he will happily reel off at will. He loves learning, and loves finding out about something new in his field – the more obscure the better – and he struggles to understand why anyone *wouldn't* want to memorise the names of all the tanks from World War II. He wants to share this information with others, and honestly thinks the project manager really wants to know, in rich technical detail, how things are going in the lab today. If the office is near an airport, he will be genuinely excited about the types of plane flying over that morning, and he has your best interests at heart as he fills you in on these details at length, with breathless excitement.

I have been saying 'he' all this time because the Typical Engineer is also white, male, and middle-aged.

When I left school and started studying electronic engineering, I had no idea what lay ahead. I'd chosen electronics pretty much on a whim, because I had a vague idea it would involve robots, and who doesn't want to learn how to make robots?

So I arrived at uni, got started on my course (Electronics

and Electrical Engineering) and pretty soon realised that hey, this stuff was interesting!

Before long I was learning how to design and analyse circuits, how to write software, how high-speed communications work (Wi-Fi, mobile networks, the internet), how you can transmit information using voltages and currents, how power networks carry electricity all over the country, and other things so fundamental to our modern lives that I couldn't believe I had never known about them before.

I had fascinating and memorable lecturers. I got along well with my classmates. We were given interesting, practical projects to do. And, step by step, I was learning a useful, fascinating skill almost from scratch.

The gender mix was a bit unbalanced, being only 10 per cent female, but 10 per cent is enough – I was rarely the only girl in the room. And my classmates were a mixed bunch anyway, coming from all over the world and from very varied backgrounds, and they were a sociable, funny, noisy and supportive group.

When, at parties for instance, people asked me what I was studying, they always seemed a bit surprised (and occasionally dubious) when I told them. The usual answer was something along the lines of 'Oh, that's a bit ... er ... different. You don't strike me as a typical engineer.'

This never really bothered me: after years of being a teenager and just wanting to fit in, it was quite invigorating to stand out. The next time I met the person from the party, they remembered: 'Oh yes, you were doing engineering.'

Engineering being a practical subject, there was a lot of emphasis on getting work experience, so halfway through the course I started doing placements in an engineering company. On these placements, I began to get to know the engineers who were out designing real circuits and working on cutting-edge new designs. I learned about working on live projects, interacting with the rest of a large team, meeting time and cost objectives, and how temperamental the office coffee machine can be.

I also learned that not all engineers are Typical Engineers. Not even close. In fact very few indeed have all the traits listed above, and those who do manifest them in different ways. The Typical Engineer above is an 'epitome', or an accumulation of generalisations based on my observations. A less kind word might be 'stereotype'. But my experience is that even a stereotype can carry some truth, and many engineers will display a subset of these characteristics.

But even if the genuine Typical Engineer is rare, there is a strong belief that this Typical Engineer is somehow the best engineer, the real engineer, the apex of what it means to not merely work in engineering, but really *be* an engineer to the core. When I started in the job and heard these stories about real engineers, the sort that I should strive to become, I found it disconcerting and off-putting. I was quite sure I didn't *want* to be that kind of person.

I did learn one important lesson though: people may expect you to fit a certain stereotype, but you don't have to cooperate. Maybe as a woman, standing out by default in the industry, I learned that more quickly. Being in a profession with so few women might mean that you are seen as a bit of an oddity, a pioneer of some sort. Luckily, I'm not. It was the generation of women before me who had to cope with being the only girl in the class, the first female engineer hired by their company, the first woman in the lab. A lot of them had to fight to make their voices heard, even to be allowed to participate. They were the ones who really broke new ground, and my generation have to be grateful to them.

In fact, by and large, I've found being female makes my job easier. People often assume I am more organised, have better social skills and am more likely to get things done simply because I'm female – stereotypes can be useful too! And most groups, and project teams, are more than happy to have someone a bit different turn up. You can bring a fresh perspective, and shake things up with new ideas. As a woman, you are almost guaranteed to fall outside the norm of the group of engineers you work in. But it is exactly this difference that can be your biggest strength. Engineering is a meritocracy, and in the end your peers will judge you on your work and on your results.

Engineering firms are crying out for engineers: there just aren't enough coming through the school system to satisfy demand. In order to effectively target and address the problems that affect all of society, we should aim to have an engineering workforce that reflects the population as a whole; at the moment, it doesn't. While there are many ways in which engineering could improve its diversity, the most striking is the gender divide. Women, while making up roughly 50 per cent of the population, make up only 6 per cent of the engineering workforce in the UK.

Engineering is a discipline that combines the precision of science with the creativity and unpredictability of art. It's interesting, surprisingly accessible once you start, and above all fun! So you can tell any girls you know who might be interested: 'No, you're not a Typical Engineer – but you could be a great one!'

A lady, went into a pet shop to buy a rare exotic animal, one that no one else had. When she told the storekeeper what she wanted, he proceeded to show her everything that he had in the line of rare and exotic animals. After much distress, the lady hadn't found anything quite unusual enough to suit her taste. She made one last plea to the storekeeper. Out of desperation, the storekeeper said, 'I do have one animal left that you haven't seen yet; however, I am somewhat reluctant to show it to you.' 'Oh, please do,' cried the lady.

So the storekeeper went back into the backroom of the store, and after a little bit returned with a cage. Putting the cage on the counter, the storekeeper proceeded to open the cage and take out the animal and set it on the counter. The lady looked, but all she saw was a piece of fur, not a head or a tail, no eyes, nothing. 'What in the world is that thing?' said the lady. 'It's a furburger,' said the storekeeper very nonchalantly. 'But what does it do?' asked the lady. 'Watch very carefully, madam,' said the storekeeper. Then the storekeeper looked down at the furburger and said, 'Furburger, the wall!' And immediately the animal flew over and hit the wall like a ton of bricks, completely destroying the wall and leaving nothing but dust. Then, just as swiftly as before, the furburger flew back and sat on the counter again. Then the storekeeper said, 'Furburger, the door!' And immediately the animal flew over and hit the door like a ton of bricks, completely demolishing the entire door and doorframe. Then, just as quickly as before, the furburger flew back and sat on the counter.

'I'll take it,' said the lady. 'All right, if you really want it,' said the storekeeper. And so, as the lady was leaving the store with her furburger, the storekeeper said, 'Pardon me, ma'am, but what are you going to do with your furburger?' And the lady looked back and said, 'Well, I've been having trouble with my husband lately, and so tonight when I get home, I'm going to put the furburger in the middle of the kitchen floor. And when my husband comes home from work, he will come in the door and look down and say to me, "What the hell is that?" and I'm going to say, "Why, dear, that's a furburger." And my husband will look at me and say, "Furburger, my ass!"'

'*The Furburger*', North American fairy tale

Once upon a time there was a brilliant and beautiful princess, so sensitive that the death of a moth could distress her for weeks on end. Her family knew of no solution. Advisers wrung their hands, sages shook their heads, brave kings left unsatisfied. So it happened for many years, until one day, out walking in the forest, the princess came to the hut of an old hunchback who knew the secrets of magic. This ancient creature perceived in the princess a woman of great energy and resourcefulness.

'My dear,' she said, 'you are in danger of being burned by your own flame.'

The hunchback told the princess that she was old, and wished to die, but could not because of her many responsibilities. She had in her charge a small village of homely people, to whom she was adviser and friend. Perhaps the princess would like to take over? Her duties would be:

1) To milk the goats
2) To educate the people
3) To compose songs for their festivals

To assist her she would have a three-legged stool and all the books belonging to the hunchback. Best of all, the old woman's harmonium, an instrument of great antiquity and four octaves. The princess agreed to stay and forgot all about the palace and the moths. The old woman thanked her, and died at once.

Jeanette Winterson, Oranges are Not the Only Fruit

ISLAM IS MY FEMINISM AND FEMINISM IS MY ISLAM

Maysa Haque

All I've ever wanted is to have a pet cat and to be a good Muslim girl. Since the former goal is a complicated long-term commitment, I've been trying to realise the latter. Unfortunately what could have been a beautiful, lifelong relationship was cut short during my childhood, when my mother refused to trade in my allergy-afflicted father for a cat. Since we kept my dad, I was raised in a large, loud and loving Muslim family. Consequently, my relationship with Islam was never cut short and continues to evolve. Though my childhood pray-and-don't-lie understanding of how to be a good Muslim girl is gradually morphing into a more complex lifestyle, my love of cats remains unchanged.

Islam provided me with my first foray into feminism through hijab, the head-covering worn by some Muslim women. I decided that I wanted to cover after attending a leadership retreat for North American Muslim youth. Having already hit puberty, I was informed by the experts that God unequivocally required me to cover my hair. I took their word for it. Obviously I needed God to like me so I could go to heaven. It was five years since 9/11, and even though I lived in a small Canadian city with a minuscule Muslim population, I felt the pressure to counteract the stigma surrounding Islam. Aside from pleasing God, for me to don hijab was to raise the battle flag against stereotype and be recognised as a beacon of unoppressed good citizenship, a counter-narrative to the negative image of my religion, especially concerning women. I was twelve years old.

I was unable to convey these sentiments to my mother, however, who covered her hair like all of my adult female relatives. She discouraged me from taking what I saw as a step towards salvation and positive Muslim public relations. I was too young. I would bring unnecessary hardship on myself. I did not understand the full social and political implications of what I was doing. She was right. But I felt strongly that I was making a well-informed choice, the right choice. She gave me my space, and I started covering my hair later, in high school. I was damn pleased with myself. I had become the parabolic wrapped candy, oystered pearl and guarded gem, topped off with a vague sense of moral superiority and self-righteousness. My feminism was hijab, and my hijab was my Islam.

The initial years of my hijab fervour saw me through high school, during which my master plan of scholastic success and community service unfolded beautifully, though without discernibly impacting the national image of Muslim women. While veiled, I was conscious that my actions could influence how people viewed Muslims, so I was always on my best behaviour. I did not want strangers to see me do something terrible in public, like jaywalk or litter, and then write all Muslims off as barbarians. I took the burden of representing Islam seriously. Fortunately, my family and friends appreciated me regardless of my garb, so what small changes occurred after I started covering were either in the public sphere or in my own head.

Along with the silly questions that all hijab-wearers face, I started getting public attention of a mixed variety. Sometimes it was positive. People would ask me about Islam, citing my unusual approachability. But suddenly strangers began to marvel at how I had mastered English, my mother tongue. They welcomed me to the country of my birth, curious about where I was 'really' from. They gently informed me that I did not have to dress 'like that' in their free nation. Although I tried not to let these well-intentioned comments get to me, they were cumulatively grating.

My original motivation for wearing hijab was being worn down and disconnected from my spirituality, and the veil metaphors that I had once celebrated now seemed demeaning. Since I spent so much time projecting my strait-laced Muslim girl image, I attempted a muted teenage rebellion in the form of brightly dyed hair and multiple piercings. My parents were puzzled. And though the dichotomy in my appearance later alarmed my university roommates, this strategy proved ineffective as I continued to cover in public.

Another difficult concept that I had learned from the Muslim community was 'gender relations'. I was taught that interactions with the opposite sex should be purposeful, public and limited, in order to protect my purity. This was a problem. I attended a public French-immersion school, where I was one of few Muslim, brown-skinned students until high school. Guiltily, I ignored the rules, and had mostly non-Muslim friends, male and female alike. This restrictive and heteronormative model of gender relations disintegrated when I made close queer friends in university and abroad. I got involved with LGBTQ+ friendly mosques in Toronto and Marseilles, where the emphasis is placed on personhood, rather than segregated sisterhood. I stopped feeling guilty over my inability to make 'good Muslim' friends, realising that 'good' does not mean Muslim, and that 'Muslim' does not mean good. My friends are lovely people who care for me, which is more important than gender, sexual orientation or religion.

My university environment promoted critical thinking, independent learning and the chance to move out on my own. Although hijab was often in the media and on my head, it was only then that I starting investigating it. In doing the research that my mom had encouraged me to do long before, I concluded that covering my hair was not the unwritten sixth pillar of Islam. A piece of cloth would not make me good or earn me God's approval.

I discovered an incredible movement of gender-inclusive Qur'anic interpretation, and queer-friendly Islamic theology. I found a version of Islam that intersected with feminism, promoting moral agency and the responsibility to uphold social justice, validating my own vague sentiments. This reshaped my worldview. I could participate in communities based on spirituality and inclusive theology, developed through critical engagement with scripture and the value of human dignity. I gained a new respect for my religion as navigable path, rather than a patriarchal monolith.

I was inadvertently relieved of my mission towards positive Muslim PR via hijab in the third year of my undergrad, which I have spent abroad in France. The situation of Muslims in France is completely different from that in North America, and it was not my responsibility as a Canadian to tackle it. Although it is legal to wear hijab in public universities such as the one I attended, the administration advised me not to, citing the possibility of discrimination from faculty members. This was considered normal. I usually did not cover my hair at school, and I often did when I went out. There were times when I preferred to cover because I received less sexual harassment, and other times when uncovering was helpful to avoid religious discrimination. Regardless, I am still in the process of renegotiating my relationship with hijab, but I have learned that it does not personally connect me with God or make me a better Muslim.

This past year in France, I have been grappling with anger against my amplified experiences of racism, sexual harassment and religious prejudice; this has taught me two important lessons. Firstly, I now understand that although improving the image of Muslim women is important, it is a sadly narrow vision of both Islam and feminism, especially when the situation of women – Muslim or not – requires colossal work. Secondly, I have been learning not to compromise my mental health over the opinions of others. Changing the mentalities of those around me is not always possible.

I do not have it all figured out yet, but I am making progress. I am thankful to God, my parents, family and friends for helping me make it this far in twenty years. I look forward to the life I have ahead of me to grow up, make mistakes and readjust my values. Though I am currently a transient student, in the Islamic tradition I prefer to call myself a seeker of knowledge. This year I have learned to live independently an ocean away from home, and have had the privilege of visiting eleven different countries. Next year I plan to study classical Arabic in Jordan. In the long term I hope to re-establish myself as a community member, where I can help to teach, engage in activism and contribute to academia. This is my life and the lifestyle that I aspire towards. I am already a good Muslim woman. This is my Islam. This is my feminism. And with the grace of God, perhaps someday I will also have a pet cat.

I believe it's a woman's right to decide what she wants to wear and if a woman can go to the beach and wear nothing, then why can't she also wear everything?

Malala Yousafzai

In March 1970, I went to the Alternate U on Sixth Avenue and 14th Street in New York City to register for a course on compulsive eating and self-image – women only … The call for the course had seemed to me almost like a travesty – feminists concerned about how they looked! … We were ostensibly happy in our blue jeans and work shirts. We were not used to discussing clothes or body size with our female friends; there was, in fact, a widespread feeling of relief that we could relax in our clothes and bodies and not worry about what was especially fashionable, provocative or appealing. We wore the clothes of rebellion and did not care what others thought. Or did we? …

… We were a self-help group at a time when energy from the women's liberation movement sparked us all into rethinking many previously held assumptions. The creativity of the movement prepared a fertile soil in which feminist ideas, nurtured and developed in countless consciousness-raising groups, in mass marches and demonstrations, in organised political campaigns, found new applications and usefulness. Compulsive eating was one such area.

Compulsive eating is a very painful and, on the surface, self-destructive activity. But feminism has taught us to be wary of this label. Feminism has taught us that activities that appear to be self-destructive are invariably adaptations, attempts to cope with the world. In our group, we turned our strongly held ideas about dieting and thinness upside down ... Slowly and unsurely we stopped dieting. Nothing terrible happened. My world did not collapse ... maybe we did not want to be thin. I dismissed that out of hand. Of course I wanted to be thin, I would be ... The dots turned out to hold the answer. Who I would be thin was different from who *I* was ... Why was I afraid of being thin? The things I was frightened of came into vision. I confronted them, always asking myself – how would it help to be fat in this situation ... As the image of my fat and thin personality conflated, I began to lose weight. I felt a deep satisfaction that I could be a size that felt good for me and no longer obsessed with food. I promised myself I would not be responsible for depriving myself of the food I liked. I had learned a crucial lesson – that I could be the same person thin as I was fat.

Susie Orbach, Fat Is A Feminist Issue

Then that little man in black there, he says women can't have as much rights as men, 'cause Christ wasn't a woman! Where did your Christ come from? From God and a woman! Man had nothing to do with Him.

If the first woman God ever made was strong enough to turn the world upside down all alone, these women together ought to be able to turn it back, and get it right side up again! And now they is asking to do it, the men better let them.

Sojourner Truth

STARING AT THE CEILING: IT'S NOT ALWAYS AS SIMPLE AS YES OR NO

Abigail Matson-Phippard

When I graduated from university I decided that I wanted to put my feminism into action, to put my money where my mouth was and try to make a difference. I found out about my local Rape Crisis Centre and signed up to volunteer at the drop-in, where survivors of rape or childhood sexual abuse would come for emotional support and to talk about their experiences. Parts of the training were emotional and difficult, looking at the effects of sexual violence and the harmful rape myths that pervade our society, but it was also deeply inspiring and motivating to be surrounded by so many amazing women all striving to counter these effects. For my first few shifts I was nervous, not knowing what to expect, but I slowly started to settle in and find my feet. The women who came to the drop-in varied greatly and came from all walks of life, but they also shared many similarities. I listened to women talk about their anxiety and anger, about how sad and hopeless they felt, about how they felt so ashamed and to blame for what had happened, and how they felt unable to speak out about their experiences, be it to the police or even to their family and friends. I heard stories about paedophile rings, ritual abuse in cults and religious groups, psychological and sexual abuse that made my skin crawl, violent gang rapes, near-death experiences at the hands of partners, and I began to truly realise that this stuff isn't just what happens in media storms and horror films, it had happened to the women I was sitting next to.

Alongside some of the more shocking stories, there were other women who came to us unsure and confused; who came in saying they weren't sure if they were in the right place, if they deserved to be here, if what had happened to them was 'bad enough' for them to be entitled to ask for help. There were many factors that made these women question themselves so much: perhaps a lack of memory about what had happened, a complex and manipulative relationship, or overwhelming feelings of responsibility for what had happened. Listening to these women stirred questions and feelings in me that I had turned away from; it made me start to think back to my own past and reflect on times when I had done things that I hadn't really wanted to do.

I remember one evening speaking to a young woman who was starting to understand that her previous boyfriend had been abusive towards her. She described how he had been emotionally abusive and manipulative, frequently coercing her into having sex with him when she didn't want to. As she spoke, my stomach twisted as it triggered memories and feelings of an ex-boyfriend of mine who had treated me very similarly. I remembered how, early on in the relationship, I had said that I wasn't in the mood to have sex and he responded by telling me that I was his girlfriend and if I loved him I should always want to have sex with him. I remembered another time when he had shouted at me for bursting into tears during sex because I had made him feel guilty, or one morning when I tried to pretend that I was still asleep – not that that seemed to deter him all that much. I like to think that he wouldn't have held me down forcibly if I had tried to stop him, but he would make it so difficult for me to say no – by starting such a big argument, or by being so cruel – that I learned that often it was easier to let him have sex with me.

Thinking back, I didn't do this only with him: there were times afterwards with other people where I would have sex with them instead of trying to find a way to say no, having that awkward conversation and risking hurting their ego, because from previous experience this hadn't gone well. So instead, I would disengage, I would look away or stare at the ceiling, offering myself as a hole for them to use. There were so many times when I had had sex and it did nothing for me; often it just hurt.

Some years after this I entered into a relationship with someone who consistently and actively sought to establish not just my consent, but that I really *wanted* to, and he didn't just do this most of the time, but every single time. This was new to me, and in the light of this the shadows of my past encounters grew longer. What I had taken to be normal didn't really seem OK any more. However, I found it difficult to find the language to explain my experiences in terms of consent or rape, because on some occasions I did, to some extent, consent: I would choose to go for that option rather than say no and risk my partner getting angry, or sometimes I would desperately try to have sex with my boyfriend, not for my own enjoyment, but to atone or say sorry, to try to show that I did love him. If I was talking to someone else about similar experiences, maybe I would use words such as 'rape', 'sexual violence' or 'coercion', but when it comes to me I move positions and shift responsibility from myself to the other as I alternate in outward anger or inward self-blame.

Another reason that I find it so hard to speak about my experiences in terms of sexual violence is because some of my previous partners are still my friends; I still like them as people and care about them. As a society we tend to portray perpetrators of sexual violence as strangers in dark alleyways, evil monsters or psychos, and much as I know that this is far from the truth, I am still reluctant to label people that I care about in this way. I found myself in a position where I could label them a rapist and in doing so connote all the horrible associations that come with it, or I could turn away from it, deny it and keep them as my friend. I saw this conflict play out again and again in the media, where the public would retaliate furiously at allegations made against their son, brother, partner or idol, refusing to accept that they could be a rapist and all that came with it. I also saw it in individuals who refused to look at or question their own actions, and in doing so kept a safe distance between themselves and the trope of the rapist as evil violent monster.

Some might argue that the people I slept with couldn't have known that I didn't really want to or that I wasn't enjoying it; surely it was my responsibility to have told them or said no. I am also aware that my own self-esteem and self-worth have had complex parts to play in what I have chosen to do with my body. I recognise too the influence of messages society has given me about what, as a woman, I should define my self-worth by: I grew up in a society that taught me to be attractive and sexy, to shave and pluck my body hair, to wear the right things, to be good in bed and please men sexually – basically to be as fuckable as possible and to define my worth by this.

But others might argue that these partners could have asked me if I wanted to, they could have properly checked to make sure that I did. I feel there is too much focus on negative consent and whether the person said no, when really we should be asking did the person say yes; I truly want this. I don't want to be patronising and assume that any of my ex-partners would have been unable to read my body language if they had tried; I think it would have been fairly obvious that I was being passive and unresponsive, looking away from them and barely engaging, as opposed to being turned on and excited, tuned in to what was happening and actively engaging with them. I worry that a lot of men don't even bother to look for enthusiasm in their sexual partners and aren't particularly concerned whether it is there; we are constantly surrounded by messages that encourage men and boys to see women as there for their own sexual gratification whilst simultaneously shaming women away from embracing their own sexuality.

I don't feel it is just an issue of yes or no; it isn't always so black and white, and it isn't always about somebody consciously deciding to rape someone; but if someone doesn't consciously decide to do it, or does it without even being immediately aware of it, is it still sexual violence? If someone runs into a crowded room swinging their arms around and as a result punches someone in the face, is it still assault? We might say no, because they didn't mean to do it, but then we might also say that they were reckless in their behaviour and it should have been obvious that their actions could hurt someone. Sexual violence and rape aren't about sex, they are about power and control; if someone feels entitled to use another person's body for their own sexual gratification then they prioritise their own needs over the other person's in an unequal power dynamic. This is why, although sexual violence can be perpetrated by anyone towards anyone, it is perpetrated most frequently by men towards women: because patriarchal structures in society encourage men to prioritise their own needs over others' and to see women as sexual objects that they are entitled to use in order to satisfy these needs. I feel that saying survivors of sexual violence had control or a choice over what happened to them is to misunderstand how power is distributed in our society and what the conditions of having choice are.

I don't feel I was taught how to make empowered choices about sex; I knew what went where, how to avoid getting an STI or getting myself pregnant, but I had no idea about how to explore my own sexuality, how to speak about sex or how to ask for what I did or didn't want. I wasn't told what an abusive relationship looked like, or a healthy one; I didn't know what constituted sexual violence – and often I don't think my sexual partners did either. From speaking to other women and reflecting on my own past experiences I have come to realise that there are a huge number of women and girls who think that sexual violence is normal; we come to both accept it and expect it, often without acknowledging it for what it is.

Somewhere in the grey area between saying yes or no is that murky water filled with hurt and uncertainties that we need to illuminate with honest conversations about sex, power and sexual violence, and a willingness to look at our own actions and how they affect other people. We cannot change and prevent sexual violence if we don't take a collective responsibility for what we lie about and cover up, and for what we neglect to turn towards because we find it too difficult to look at and accept.

I am an example of what is possible when girls from the very beginning of their lives are loved and nurtured by people around them.

I was surrounded by extraordinary women in my life who taught me about quiet strength and dignity.

Michelle Obama

My mom brought me up to be a feminist. She would always point out to my brother and me that our culture does often portray women like objects. For example, we would always watch Lakers games as a family, but my mom would always point out every time the cheerleaders come on, 'OK, so look, here's the story that gets told: the men get to be the heroic skilled athletes and the women just get to be pretty.' She didn't mean any offence to any individual woman who was working as a cheerleader, but she wanted me and my brother to be aware of it because we see these images on TV, in the movies, and on magazines all the time. And if you don't stop and think about it, it just sort of seeps into your brain and that becomes the way you perceive reality. I do call myself a feminist. Absolutely! It's worth paying attention to the roles that are sort of dictated to us and that we don't have to fit into those roles. We can be anybody we wanna be.

Joseph Gordon-Levitt

Motherhood can shift your perspective and intensify your emotions. It can bring out your creativity and ingenuity, your desire to do good, or even just a desire to do *more*. It can spark ideas, redefine what's 'important' in your life, and ultimately change you – in ways you never expected.

Michelle Horton

There is an unspoken pact that women are supposed to follow. I am supposed to act like I constantly feel guilty about being away from my kids. (I don't. I love my job.) Mothers who stay at home are supposed to pretend they are bored and wish they were doing more corporate things. (They don't. They love their job.) If we all stick to the plan there will be less blood in the streets.

Amy Poehler, Yes Please

... a mother, labouring under a portion of the misery, which the constitution of society seems to have entailed on all her kind[.] It is, my child, my dearest daughter, only such a mother, who will dare to break through all restraint to provide for your happiness – who will voluntarily brave censure herself, to ward off sorrow from your bosom. From my narrative, my dear girl, you may gather the instruction, the counsel, which is meant rather to exercise than influence your mind. – Death may snatch me from you, before you can weigh my advice, or enter into my reasoning: I would then, with fond anxiety, lead you very early in life to form your grand principle of action, to save you from the vain regret of having, through irresolution, let the spring-tide of existence pass away, unimproved, unenjoyed. – Gain experience – ah! gain it – while experience is worth having, and acquire sufficient fortitude to pursue your own happiness; it includes your utility, by a direct path ... Had I not wasted years in deliberating, after I ceased to doubt, how I ought to have acted – I might now be useful and happy.

Mary Wollstonecraft, Maria, or The Wrongs of Woman

The twentysomething years are an incredible time for self-growth and self-discovery. It's a time to define our adulthood and ourselves. So many people assume that the only way to 'find yourself' is alone, in the woods, in solitary introspection.

But, in my experience, there's nothing quite as introspective as motherhood. It'll hold a mirror right up to your flaws, your shortcomings, your deep-set issues. Seeing yourself – seeing life, in general – through the lens of a new life can be quite transformative. It's given me an urgent reason to grow up and be my best self.

Michelle Horton

FOR OUR CHILDREN, FOR OUR MOTHERS, FOR ALL STILL STRUGGLING: WE MUST SAVE THE HUMAN RIGHTS ACT

Rosie Brighouse

If you've seen the headlines in recent months, you'll know the government is bent on repealing the Human Rights Act – the law that, since 1998, has let ordinary people hold the state to account. Every day, my colleagues and I use the Act to help our clients seek justice, so it won't come as a monumental surprise that I oppose its repeal. A belief in feminism is indivisible from a belief in human rights – and every feminist in the UK should be opposed too.

The government wants to replace the HRA with a 'British Bill of Rights', which will limit the use of human rights law to the 'most serious cases', with the 'trivial' dismissed outright. An elderly woman waits hours to use the toilet in her dying days. A mother is spied on by council officials when she's falsely accused of lying about her address. Rosa Parks refuses to go to the back of the bus. Should politicians be allowed to decide where the line between 'trivial' and 'serious' human rights abuses lies?

If we allow partisan politicians to erode the universality of human rights, all our rights protections will be diminished – and the vulnerable will be hardest hit. As history shows, the most vulnerable are often women, disadvantaged by lack of wealth, power or agency. This remains true today, where modern slavery, domestic and sexual violence, trafficking, pay inequality and lack of public representation exist in a climate of 'everyday sexism' that touches every woman in the country.

Gender injustice is the oldest and most entrenched injustice on the planet. Even in the UK, it's so engrained in our day-to-day existence that we sometimes stop seeing it. The HRA helps focus the glare of injustice on those commonplace inequalities. This simple piece of legislation has been used to challenge unfair decisions to remove children from mothers, seek protection for domestic-violence victims, defend the dignity of women in care and safeguard asylum-seeking women.

It's a constant reminder to the powerful that, if they

neglect and abuse the vulnerable, the vulnerable can fight back. That can be inconvenient for those at the top – which perhaps explains this clamour for repeal.

Crucially, the HRA puts a positive obligation on the state to prevent human rights violations; sticking their heads in the sand isn't enough. It's forced public bodies to improve guidance and policies to ensure everybody is treated with dignity, fairness and respect. It makes it much harder for injustices against the voiceless – those on the margins of society, whose opinions might not be quite as important to vote-chasing politicians – to be swept under the carpet.

I am a solicitor at Liberty, a campaigning group working to protect civil liberties and promote human rights in the UK through a combination of test-case litigation, lobbying, campaigning and free advice. Liberty represents Mary (not her real name) from the Democratic Republic of Congo, who was abducted by men calling themselves security officers in 2012. She was held for weeks, subjected to regular gang rape and tortured. Eventually she escaped, fled the DRC and arrived in the UK. She was taken to Yarl's Wood, locked up for weeks and monitored by male officers. She developed symptoms of post-traumatic stress disorder and her pre-existing mental health problems worsened. We're using the HRA to seek a declaration that Mary was unlawfully detained – and hopefully to make sure this doesn't happen again.

Although it's not what some MPs and newspapers would have us believe, countless 'ordinary people' have found justice using the HRA – young and old, wealthy and poor, male and female. But many human rights issues still disproportionately affect women, particularly issues of sexual abuse and domestic violence. People often believe police have a legal obligation to investigate these crime; in fact, only the HRA imposes a legal and effective duty on them properly to investigate serious offences. Contrary to many people's expectations, the police cannot be sued for negligence when things go wrong, and the HRA is often victims' only route to justice.

For example, a young woman called Joanna Michael was brutally murdered by her ex-partner in front of her two young children in 2009. She called police twice on the night she died – her nearest police station was minutes from her house – but they erroneously downgraded her first call. By the time officers finally arrived, Joanna was dead. The Supreme Court upheld a longstanding rule that victims cannot sue the police for negligence – but ruled that they *could* seek justice using the HRA, the only legal route available to them.

The HRA protects the rights of women where our centuries-old legal system, long dominated by men and men's priorities, fails to do so. A client of Liberty wanted to stop the police returning intimate photos of her young daughters to the man convicted of sexual offences against one of the girls. The archaic, Victorian law of property told the police they had to do so – he owned the items on which the photos were stored, end of story. Liberty stepped in and, using the HRA, showed their rights were more important.

There are so many cases in which the HRA has proved the only recourse to justice for survivors of domestic and sexual violence – far too many to mention. The victims of taxi driver John Worboys – who raped and sexually assaulted more than a hundred women – could only take action against the bungling Metropolitan Police by challenging them under the HRA, for example. And after police failed to investigate the rapist of a seventeen-year-old girl because they were too busy falsely accusing her of lying – driving her to self-harm and attempted suicide – she was only able to seek compensation using the HRA.

On paper, our society no longer tolerates domestic violence or marital rape – but these things still happen. No other law can protect women's rights in the same way. And no other law has the flexibility to be used as effectively against the new challenges facing women and girls today: 'sexting' among children, 'revenge porn', aggressive trolling of women who dare to voice opinions on social media.

There's still much to do before we have true parity between men and women around the world. The progression of universal human rights law can help to achieve such parity. The government's short-sighted and destructive anti-human rights position will undermine attempts by other women in other countries to persuade their governments to protect their fundamental rights. Scrapping the

HRA would be a colossal step backwards – if the British government doesn't value human rights standards, why should any other oppressive patriarchal government feel the need to change? For our children, for our mothers, for all who still struggle for basic rights around the world, we must get behind the fight for the HRA – because we won't know what we've got till it's gone.

There is a war on our planet, bigger than all other wars. It is a war against little girls living in Africa, Asia, the USA, Canada, Europe, Australia and South America ... We mourn three million victims of female genital mutilation (FGM) every year ... FGM breaches all human rights and has no place in any twenty-first-century society. Let us take serious action!

Waris Dirie

I am a woman with thoughts and questions and shit to say. I say if I'm beautiful. I say if I'm strong. You will not determine my story – I will.

Amy Schumer

Male fantasies, male fantasies, is everything run by male fantasies? Up on a pedestal or down on your knees, it's all a male fantasy: that you're strong enough to take what they dish out, or else too weak to do anything about it. Even pretending you aren't catering to male fantasies is a male fantasy: pretending you're unseen, pretending you have a life of your own, that you can wash your feet and comb your hair unconscious of the ever-present watcher peering through the keyhole, peering through the keyhole in your own head, if nowhere else. You are a woman with a man inside watching a woman. You are your own voyeur.

Margaret Atwood, The Robber Bride

Woman's virtue is man's greatest invention.

Cornelia Otis Skinner

ARE YOU A STRIPPER OR A SHAVER?

Bertie Brandes

There's a forum gathering comments on Reddit at the moment that's made everyone I've shown it to so far, and you in about ten minutes, sink their head into their hands and let out a low, defeated groan. It's probably not what you're expecting if you know anything about Reddit already. Commonly referred to as the 'front page of the internet', this social networking site has a pretty fair reputation for being largely populated by the type of entitled, embittered men who like nothing more than obsessively rephrasing the assertion that 'feminism wants men to be second-class slaves'. It's a site where women are objectified, insulted and stigmatised, and ideas of women's rights are dismantled in a half disturbing and half entirely absurd way.

Here's a recent example: 'Sex with minors isn't allowed ... because of Western feminism wanting to control male sexuality so that young girls don't compete with them.' There's your first groan, but by no means your last.

Recently, while wading through the insanity, I clicked over to something that was depressing in a wholly new and more interesting way – a forum where mostly female Reddit users shared and discussed their earliest memories of being looked at in a sexual way. Out of the tens of thousands of comments, what was most striking but perhaps least surprising was the recurrence of the older man as the sexualiser. On the whole these were not stories of gleeful boys loitering by swings in the school playground but predatory adults burning holes with their eyes into the chests of girls with an average age of eleven or twelve. Is your head in your hands yet? Thought so.

After the initial head-banging against your nearest solid surface, this stuff generally prompts one of two discussions: either that we have a cultural problem with sexualising girls or there's an epidemic of paedophilia. I'm not sure the two aren't linked. In an essay on the BBC's Light Entertainment in the *London Review of Books*, Andrew O'Hagan questions whether British 'culture itself is largely paedophile in its commercial and entertainment excitements'. He makes a brutal point, and one that applies to the fashion–beauty industry. Clearly this is not simply a question of a few leering old men. We're living in a culture which actively encourages the idea that female bodies are a form of visual currency from an ever younger age. Regardless of the important arguments put forward by some sex-positive feminists, the imbalance in how girls and boys are encouraged to present themselves is pretty startling. Sure, as an adult or a parent you have relative freedom of choice, but in general the shorts on offer to girls will always have the option of being shorter, the T-shirts tighter, stretchier and the slogans more questionable. As a young teenage girl you will inevitably wonder at some point if maybe it's time you start wearing a thong. It's odd because, as far as I'm aware, I didn't and don't get hotter than my brother in summer or grow more hair or generally smell more or get drier lips which ... oh go on, throw a bit of a cherry tint in there why don't you? Apart from, you know, the *womb*, we're really not so very different at all – despite what the routines I was encouraged to adopt from as early as ten or eleven might imply.

Ultimately it all seems to hinge on the idea of value. Our industry-driven consumer culture, the one taking upwards of three hundred billion pounds a year out of women's pockets for beauty products, has, without our permission, placed the female body within a structure of worth that essentially implies it has a price. It's hardly surprising then that on the street we are understood as innately exhibitionist; an object to be judged, whistled at, heckled, grabbed – worse.

According to statistics published in the *Guardian* last year, four in ten girls aged between thirteen and seventeen have been coerced into sexual acts. You can't blame an epidemic of sexual violence on an invisible evil. As the Reddit forum shows, girls and young women are navigating a world inhabited by men who are invited to objectify their bodies, while simultaneously being encouraged by a complicit culture to uphold a level of maintenance and grooming that is not required from their male peers. In the summer of 2014 *Miss Vogue*, the younger sister of *Vogue* which describes itself as aimed at a 'teenage audience', ran a flow quiz about body hair that opened with the question: 'Are you a stripper or a shaver?' The feature went on to ask: 'Do you have a high pain threshold?' or 'Would you describe your hair as coarse?' and then according to your answers offered a body hair solution. What was so alarming about this quiz was that *Miss Vogue* somehow failed to include the option to leave your body hair untouched because it's fine/you might be a child/you are beautiful exactly as you are. Instead they shoved a '*Vogue* Loves' stamp on a £375 personal hair-removing laser and moved on. This kind of media nips at the heels of women from as soon as they're old enough to read. It latches on and it refuses to let up.

The thing is, while I can baulk in horror at that Reddit forum, as long as we continue to turn a blind eye to everything else we're complicit in a particularly modern form of harassment. From women's magazines to newspapers, gaming, films, TV and the infinite spaces between there is a criminal lack of effort to present girls and women in any way other than objectified or fetishised. For how long will we blindly swallow a toxic culture and then reel in shock at the reality of sexism manifest in the day-to-day? I always thought Reddit had a problem with women; I never thought it would be the place I realised I did too.

Men do not just need to stop being violent. The vast majority of men are not violent. But men do need to stop being silent. Calling violence against women, whether street harassment or sexual harassment or rape or murder, a 'women's issue' allows men to ignore it as if we have no responsibility for it or stake in ending it.

Donald McPherson

We need to stop playing Privilege or Oppression Olympics because we'll never get anywhere until we find more effective ways of talking through difference. We should be able to say, 'This is my truth,' and have that truth stand without a hundred clamouring voices shouting, giving the impression that multiple truths cannot coexist.

Roxane Gay, Bad Feminist

In my understanding, the women's movement is first and foremost about memory. It is about remembering the women who lived, who struggled, worked and loved before us, including those we have never heard about.

Elif Shafak, Fifty Shades of Feminism

CONNECTIONS ARE EVERYTHING

Laura Bates

When I started asking women about everyday sexism in early 2012, they'd often begin by telling me they only had one or two stories. But as they related their experiences, they began making connections. They'd connect those stories to others, as more and more incidents came to mind. As one woman told her story, others would be reminded of similar events, and the conversation would snowball, much as it did when I moved the Everyday Sexism Project online.

A hundred thousand testimonies later, the project has become a vast and powerful patchwork quilt of people's experiences of all forms of gender inequality, told in their own words. When I think about what has made Everyday Sexism effective, I think immediately of the connections it has wrought between individuals. Women who have carried the weight of a rape or sexual assault for years without telling anybody have written that, thanks to the sense of community they have found in other women's voices, they finally feel less alone. Some said that it was the first time they had begun to feel that what had happened was not their own fault. Some wrote that the strength of other women standing up and decrying sexism in all its forms had given them the courage to report a case of workplace discrimination or of sexual assault for the first time. The immediacy of the connections formed through social media has provided support, strength and solace, as women tweeting their experiences are met with compassionate responses from others around the world.

As well as providing catharsis and comfort for those who contribute, the expanse of data collected by the project has also revealed important truths, particularly in the form of connections between the different entries. Clear links have emerged between the entries reporting different types of gender inequality. As feminists, we are used to being told what we 'should' focus on, or scolded for 'making a fuss' about particular topics (often by male commentators). Talking about rape or domestic violence is acceptable, but mention street harassment and you're 'getting upset about nothing'. You can tackle the under-representation of women in business or politics, but woe betide you if you try to take on media sexism – you're just looking for something to be offended by. Don't you know there are more important things to worry about?

This argument is extremely thin. Feminists are quite capable of fighting on more than one front at the same time. Women's rights activists in the UK are currently battling everything from female genital mutilation to sexism and racism in music videos, and there is no reason why we shouldn't tackle every manifestation of gender inequality, no matter how apparently 'minor'. If anything, the project entries have shown how important it is to fight the smaller battles alongside the big.

The same sexist slurs hurled at women who are told 'not to make a fuss' are also used by a man abusing his partner behind closed doors. A woman who tries to ignore her street harasser finds that he pursues her home and sexually assaults her on her own doorstep. One 'type' of incident often escalates into another. It quickly becomes clear that it is futile to tackle the disparity between the numbers of male and female MPs without taking into account the fact that new female Cabinet ministers are accused of parading down the Downing Street 'catwalk' or described as 'Cameron's Cuties', their clothes and make-up picked over by a sexist press. The ideas and attitudes that proliferate if we allow the treatment of women as second-class citizens in one sphere have a knock-on impact on behaviour towards them elsewhere. And so we must tackle gender inequality in all its forms.

The second kind of connection that emerged from the

project entries was that between different kinds of prejudice. We were receiving stories from women who weren't just experiencing sexism, but sexism intermingled and combined with other forms of discrimination. Older women described being ignored, or dismissed as 'batty'. Black women were told they were 'spicy' or 'exotic', or asked to twerk. Asian women faced stereotypes about obedient wives and mail-order brides. Women with mental health problems were accused of being 'hysterical' or over-reacting. Disabled women were asked to pole dance around walking sticks, and faced jibes about 'female drivers' in their wheelchairs. Trans women were assaulted and driven from public bathrooms. Lesbian couples were hounded by men asking to 'watch' or 'join in'. Bisexual, asexual, queer and intersex women were doubted, ridiculed or accused of being 'greedy'. Larger women were told they should be grateful for sexual assault. Sex workers who experienced assaults were told what happened to them couldn't be classified as rape.

It quickly became clear that, like the different 'types' of sexism, these separate inequalities aren't experienced in conveniently neat, individual ways, but intersect and combine to have a cumulative impact. And it became clear that in order to fight one it was necessary to take them all into account, integrated into the fight – to recognise that sexism doesn't exist in a vacuum, but intertwined with a range of other prejudices, all part of being different, or 'other', from the default, dominant societal norm.

The third type of connections were between the project entries reported by women and those that came from men. Instead of separate, distinct problems, they were clearly describing two sides of the same coin. We heard from men who were laughed at when they asked for parental leave and women denied promotions because they were considered a 'maternity risk'. From girls who were called hysterical drama queens while their male peers were taught that 'boys don't cry'. From fathers who were congratulated for 'babysitting' their own children and mothers who were criticised for 'taking a night off'. The entries made it very clear that fighting against outdated gender stereotypes would have a beneficial impact for everybody, not just for women. That it was not a case of people experiencing different problems according to their sex, but rather many people (though predominantly women) suffering from the negative impact of the same sexist norms. That it was in everybody's interest to fight this battle together – not a case of men 'against' women, or women 'against' men, but of people standing together against prejudice.

These different links lead, inevitably, to another kind of connection: the power of people standing together. There is so much we could change if we unite and support one another – to fight injustice and prejudice of every kind, on every level – and to see sexism and sexual violence not as a 'woman's issue', but as a human rights issue.

All this plays a part in my feminism. I call myself a

feminist because everybody should be treated equally, regardless of sex. I call myself a feminist because others stand alongside me and I am proud to stand with them. I call myself a feminist because in pursuit of equality we should fight every battle, no matter how small. I call myself a feminist because there are structures of inequality still operating on the grounds of sex, race, class, sexuality, gender orientation, disability and more; and they are waiting to be dismantled. I call myself a feminist because it is in everybody's interest to treat human beings with fairness, dignity and respect.

I call myself a feminist because it is not a scary word. What's scary is the fact that one in three women on the planet will be raped or beaten in her lifetime. What's scary is the world of inequality that feminism exists to fix.

You may not control all the events that happen to you, but you can decide not to be reduced by them.

Maya Angelou, Letter to my Daughter

She might, in fact, go crazy, as has happened to a lot of people who break rules. Not the people who play at rebellion but really only solidify their already dominant positions in society … but those who take some larger action that disrupts the social order. Who try to push through the doors that are usually closed to them. They do sometimes go crazy, these people, because the world is telling them not to want the things they want. It can seem saner to give up – but then one goes insane from giving up.

E. Lockhart, The Disreputable History of Frankie Landau-Banks

In my early twenties, the 'spinster wish' was my private shorthand for the novel pleasures of being alone. As I grew older, and felt more strongly the cultural expectation of marriage, the words became more like a thought experiment, a way to imagine in detail what it would look like to never settle down. The word *wish* is crucial. A wish is a longing, not a plan of action. It was perhaps precisely because I found so much meaning and satisfaction in my relationships that I conjured such an escapist fantasy, not because I didn't want such relationships, but because I also wanted to find other avenues of meaning and identity.

Only now, looking back, do I see that this thought experiment ultimately doubled as positive reinforcement; by continuing to wonder about and converse, internally, with 'ambiguous women' – the scholar Carolyn Heilbrun's wonderful term for those who choose not to centre their lives around a man – I became one.

It wasn't until I researched this book and came to

a more comprehensive understanding of the largely unwritten history of the 'ambiguous woman', that I truly fell in love with the word *spinster* itself.

Kate Bolick, Spinster

THE DIFFICULT, UNDATEABLE DATING COLUMNIST

Caroline Kent

I have cultivated a persona of someone who is in control of and empowered by her choices in sex and relationships. I am glamorous and sassy and seduction is my second language. I am a dating columnist.

I am also a hypocrite because, in truth, I am difficult and I find other people difficult too.

I am the one who is supposed to be good at this. I am supposed to find relationships easy.

I admire intractable, unloveable female characters in TV or books. Women whose behaviour is repulsive and selfish entrance me. They seem far more alive and aware and unapologetic than most would ever dare to be. They're really living.

But life is not a book, where a character can be hard and horrid and unlikeable yet a benevolent author might nevertheless carve empathy into her fellow characters and redemption into her destiny.

I do not make it easy to like me. I am actively combative towards those who might dare try to love me. Making things harder than they need to be is kind of my forte. I did not grow easily into my body, or my brain. I did not blossom into womanhood, womanhood simply became another nuisance for me to deal with. And relationships were part of that. I didn't fit anywhere, with anyone. Even my own skin felt itchy, like cheap nylon I was just antsy to strip off at the end of the day.

I felt everything about my existence, physical and interpersonal, was clumsy. I took up too much space. My personality, like my body, was burdensome and bulky and did not make socialising easy.

I willed myself to shrink in every possible way: the hips that spread like melted butter when I sat down, the thoughts that spiralled out several metres from my head and engulfed me, the booming voice that led to me getting tested for hearing deficiencies (negative; turns out I just really couldn't shut the fuck up).

Growing up, huh? I don't remember becoming a woman, but I do remember when I stopped being a girl. My memory is blurred from the Malibu but I remember them holding me up because I couldn't stand. I remember the leggings I was wearing, what I had for lunch that day, the colour my bedroom walls were painted, and the last song I had danced to before I found myself outside in this group of guys a few years older. Two of them, one under either arm, a few others in the background, one laughing, one keeping look-out. The smell of clean, fresh blood that I woke up to at five a.m. I was oddly intrigued by that blood: it wasn't like the brown smear that descended monthly, this was scarlet, thick and plump and it smelled like a baby's head or the time my brother slammed a door in my face during a game of 40–40 and a stream of purple shot from my nose like the hosepipe being turned on for the first time that summer.

A month or so later and I'm making it difficult to call myself a victim by wearing a slutty outfit. At school they're handing out these special straws that block your bottles and make it difficult for guys to spike your drink. We're fifteen. Better start looking after our bottles if we don't want to ruin a good night out by getting ourselves raped. My friends giggle as I take a sharpie and scrawl 'DATE RAPE' across my knuckles like a parody of the LOVE/HATE tattoos on the fists of the punk guy I fancy. 'That's not funny,' my mum scolds as I walk in the front door, faux-tattooed fist wrapped around a mocha chip frappé. 'You don't make it easy for people to pity you, Caroline,' is implied.

I started to drink till I blacked out. To make it all less difficult. By my twenties I had learned that alcohol is less difficult than family. And then that cocaine is less difficult than alcohol. And not eating: that seemed a lot less difficult than nourishing myself. I was chasing difficult, it seemed, right into a relationship in which I was routinely abused by the man who adored me.

Going from girl to woman meant, for me, learning to apologise to the people who made me feel that I was difficult and so I did not matter quite as much. I deserved these things; it was my punishment for not making my presence easy for them to handle.

I learned to make myself (it all) look easy. Relationships, sex. I made a career from telling other people how easy it can all be if you're not difficult like me.

Feminism has always been, and is still, the only place I feel it's 'OK' that I am difficult. It's OK to be confused and yet quite sure, it's OK to be both the wounded and healer. Femininity, femin-ism, does not expect I smooth my edges or shrink to fit in its box.

I call myself a feminist even though I don't know quite what feminism is. I find it as hard to define, in truth, as I find myself. And my God, that is some sublime sort of comfort. I might not be able to write its entry in the dictionary, but I know what it feels like. I know that when I hear it speak I recognise its voice immediately. I know feminism like a deaf-blind baby knows its mother; I couldn't articulate it but I feel her presence and her comfort so intensely, and I know in some inexplicable way that it is my safety and my support. Sometimes it's the only faith I have.

It's where being difficult doesn't mean I am wrong. And maybe that's a self-indulgent and self-serving definition of something that should be about a broader societal change, but on those days when I feel like my brain would drizzle out of my nose if it didn't have my stiff upper lip to lean on, I lean on feminism.

Feminism was the voice that still whispered when all the people I had told to fuck off finally stopped trying, the voice that something deep inside me recognised when I heard it in books, in articles and on blogs, and eventually inside my own head; it was the voice that said, 'You do not deserve to be treated in this way. You did not ask for that, and you did not consent to that. You may not have known fully, consciously, what was going on, but that does not mean the things that happened to you were not wrong.' It teaches me to grow strong and gently reminds me that the more I give in to what I think is expected of me rather than what I truly want, the more my life doesn't feel like mine. I am difficult and I am OK.

Some people ask, 'Why the word *feminist*? Why not just say you are a believer in human rights, or something like that?' Because that would be dishonest. Feminism is, of course, part of human rights in general – but to choose to use the vague expression *human rights* is to deny the specific and particular problem of gender. It would be a way of pretending that it was not women who have, for centuries, been excluded. It would be a way of denying that the problem of gender targets women. That the problem was not about being human, but specifically about being a female human.

Chimamanda Ngozi Adichie

Ideally, what should be said to every child, repeatedly, throughout his or her school life is something like this: 'You are in the process of being indoctrinated. We have not yet evolved a system of education that is not a system of indoctrination. We are sorry, but it is the best we can do. What you are being taught here is an amalgam of current prejudice and the choices of this particular culture. The slightest look at history will show how impermanent these must be. You are being taught by people who have been able to accommodate themselves to a regime of thought laid down by their predecessors. It is a self-perpetuating system. Those of you who are more robust and individual than others will be encouraged to leave and find ways of educating yourself – educating your own judgements. Those that stay must remember, always, and all the time, that they are being moulded and patterned to fit into the narrow and particular needs of this particular society.'

Doris Lessing, The Golden Notebook

A prouder young woman was seldom seen than she, when, having composed herself, she electrified the family by appearing before them with the letter in one hand, the cheque in the other, announcing that she had won the prize! Of course there was a great jubilee, and when the story came every one read and praised it; though after her father had told her that the language was good, the romance fresh and hearty, and the tragedy quite thrilling, he shook his head, and said in his unworldly way—

'You can do better than this, Jo. Aim at the highest, and never mind the money.'

'*I* think the money is the best part of it. What *will* you do with such a fortune?' asked Amy, regarding the magic slip of paper with a reverential eye.

'Send Beth and Mother to the sea-side for a month or two,' answered Jo promptly …

To the sea-side they went, after much discussion; and though Beth didn't come home as plump and rosy as could be desired, she was much better, while Mrs March declared she felt ten years younger; so Jo was satisfied with the investment of her prize-money, and fell to work with a cheery spirit, bent on earning more of those delightful cheques. She did earn several that year, and began to feel herself a power in the house; for by the magic of a pen, her 'rubbish' turned into comforts for them all. 'The Duke's Daughter' paid the butcher's bill, 'A Phantom Hand' put down a new carpet, and 'The Curse of the Coventrys' proved the blessing of the Marches in the way of groceries and gowns.

Wealth is certainly a most desirable thing, but poverty has its sunny side, and one of the sweet uses of adversity, is the genuine satisfaction which comes from hearty work of head or hand; and to the inspiration of necessity, we owe half the wise, beautiful, and useful blessings of the world. Jo enjoyed a taste of this satisfaction, and ceased to envy richer girls, taking great comfort in the knowledge that she could supply her own wants, and need ask no one for a penny.

Louisa May Alcott, Little Women Wedded

Show me a woman who doesn't feel guilty and I'll show you a man.

Erica Jong, Fear of Flying

WOMEN SHOULD GET TO BE RUBBISH TOO

Isabel Adomakoh Young

I remember my Facebook newsfeed on International Women's Day 2015: lots of posts remembering, celebrating and publicising various historical women's achievements, and calling for social and political equality. I enthusiastically identify as feminist and always hope to see equality promoted, so it was exciting and encouraging to see! But something struck me as I scrolled through: it's a really bad idea to mix up achievement on the one hand and deserving equality on the other.

The thing is, while it's hugely important to celebrate impressive women's achievements (and that is partly what IWD is for), we're at risk of confusing the two, of raising women from oppressed to ideal, which can be far too easily reversed. Have a look at hilarious but scary sites like ByeFelipe and Tinder Nightmares for examples of the creepy 'romantics' who claim to put 'women on a pedestal' but turn abusive when women use that oh-so-kindly-granted pedestal power to refuse their suitors' unsolicited offers of sex ...

But it's not just nutters online – even feminist campaigns can sometimes do it. I often see supporters of, say, the 50:50 Parliament petition (which campaigns for equal representation of genders in government) saying stuff like 'if women ruled the world we'd all be much better off'. Sandi Toksvig, a few hours after announcing her founding of the Women's Equality Party (which I'm very excited about!), was pictured holding a sign that read 'Only 23% Women MPs = Unused Potential'. It's lovely that people have faith in women's abilities, and of course a positive campaign gets further than a moany one, but 'unused potential' is actually not at all the point. We should have the opportunity to fulfil our potential because it's just morally, politically and humanly right. Whether women actually do succeed depends on any number of other factors and is really not that relevant. To put it another way, society doesn't educate kids because a few get As, does it? It's because it's the good thing to do.

Take the 'Strong Female Character' trope in sci-fi and comics: it's great that writers are putting in more female characters, but frustratingly often they're either lacking depth, utterly unconnected to the plot, or both. I really like

Sophia McDougall's observation, 'Nowadays the princesses all know kung fu, and yet they're still the same princesses. They're still love interests, still the one girl in a team of five boys.' How many stories can you think of like that? Loads, I bet – just look at the poster for any ensemble action film. And it's traditional for society to demand perfection from women, although what that involves has altered through the ages: examine paintings of the ideal beauty of the 1400s and you'll find a weirdly long neck, small breasts and a big forehead – that's what society demanded back then. I think female audiences deserve to see their own fascinating, three-dimensional selves reflected in modern British culture – and men need to see them too! If we allow hollow paragons of kick-ass, sexy, irrelevant perfection to outnumber complex, dirty, envious, uncertain, cruel, even morally dubious yet sympathetic female characters, we're probably just making yet another unattainable ideal; girls will be told they're not 'feisty' enough, and Lord knows we don't need that on top of everything else.

A favourite character of mine, the Batman spin-off and fictional badass Harley Quinn, is one of the few comic-book superheroines with real depth: fans such as Tara Strand love her because 'She doesn't make choices that are smart or good for a woman, but she gets to *make* those choices. Men are allowed to be fuck-ups in all kinds of characters, and women aren't.' She is feisty, but also complex – and sometimes wrong. And best of all, she was invented not to fill a quota of representation or to show women can be amazing, but because she's funny and interesting and empathetic.

Also, social expectation of 'strength' can lead to real danger for people. For instance, black women are supposedly 'sturdy', better able to survive poverty and violence than their white counterparts. Joy Gardner, a Jamaican who died in custody while being deported from the UK, was described by one of several officers who wound thirteen feet of adhesive tape around her head and face as 'the strongest and most violent woman' he had ever encountered.

Preconceptions about the 'Strong Black Woman' in the judicial system mean they're given longer prison sentences and then treated much worse by prison officers, who assume they'll be more aggressive or rowdy than white inmates. In a recent documentary, journalists filming undercover in Yarl's Wood detention centre hear a guard call the (not even criminal) detainees 'beasties'.

The trope plays itself out in other ways too. For instance, a lovely article by Wambui Mwangi explores the impact the illusion of strength had on her seemingly invincible black mother, and asks, 'Do we ever ask ourselves what sort of toll it took on her?'

For trans women, hate-motivated attacks can often be, at least superficially, based on the idea that they should, as 'men', be able to physically fight back. We all have to think about the toll depictions of strength, without space for weakness, take on women in the real world.

It's also important to remember that men suffer from something similar, though it's from different roots: what's known as the 'hyper-masculine ideal' (the shaving foam advert-style 'real man') makes abused, 'effeminate', homosexual, insecure or physically less dominant men feel inadequate. This causes false pride, which on a more trivial level might manifest itself in the classic stereotype of being unwilling to ask for directions, but also in very serious issues such as feeling unable to seek help when they're suicidal or mentally unwell, because they're scared of seeming weak; it was reported in the *International Business Times* in February 2015 that '78 per cent of all UK suicides in 2013 were committed by men'.

I'm not saying feminist movements are about to start insulting weak women or anything, but the constant requirement to be strong, to be worthy of opportunities, to 'do it all', really can be damaging. The thing is, we're not all beautiful, strong or perfect – nor should we have to be in order to merit respect. As Sophia McDougall points out, in fiction does anyone judge addict Sherlock Holmes or psychopathic James Bond for their distance from perfection as men? Women need to remember that we don't have value because we're beautiful, or deserve equal representation because we're strong and brave, whether that's in comics or in Parliament. Many of us aren't those things and they certainly can't be tied to gender. Women and non-binary identified people need to have high-achieving representatives to look to and to hold accountable, just as men do, but we should praise and criticise them as people.

And it really is not too demanding for everyone, but especially women, to ask to be appreciated in all our complex glory and our flaws. If you attribute perfection to women you pre-condemn them for failing to live up to it. Women, including fictional women, should have the space to be boring, selfish, stupid, impatient and mean, and to be both empathised with and judged for it as people, regardless of what's under their clothes or how they identify. Same for men and everybody else. As Katharine Hepburn tells John Howard in *The Philadelphia Story*, 'I don't want to be worshipped. I want to be loved.'

What's the worst possible thing you can call a woman? Don't hold back, now.

You're probably thinking of words like slut, whore, bitch, cunt (I told you not to hold back!), skank.

Okay, now, what are the worst things you can call a guy? Fag, girl, bitch, pussy. I've even heard the term 'mangina'.

Notice anything? The worst thing you can call a girl is a girl. The worst thing you can call a guy is a girl. Being a woman is the ultimate insult. Now tell me that's not royally fucked up.

Jessica Valenti, Full Frontal Feminism

virago

1. A domineering, violent, or bad-tempered woman: '*that virago of a wife of his needs locking up*'

1.1 *archaic* A woman of masculine strength or spirit; a female warrior

Oxford Online Dictionary

The internet can empower me as much as I can let it dumb me down. I've realised it's a choice. And that I can have my cake and eat it too. I can check out the Ferguson hashtag, watch *The Trews*, read the BBC and CNN website, see if any of my friends have posted any relevant links on Facebook and then watch a video of a bunny eating a raspberry to calm me down all whilst drinking my morning coffee. This is awesome.

So anyway my next thought process was like what can I do about this stuff? What is my area of expertise and how can I take action about things that I care about and can actually help with? …

This is not about sitting online and debating whether Miley Cyrus is a good or bad example for young girls, or whether shaving your pussy is a political or personal choice. I feel very lucky that I wake up every morning and don't have to shave my toes, but I can if I want to.

Yay for me! Thank you feminism, genuinely. But I feel unhappy that still so many girls are afraid of having a voice, they are encouraged to be silenced. You can still be fired for not sleeping with your boss, women still get paid less than men, there is still sexism in the workplace, we still look down on older women that don't want to have kids, prostitutes are still criminalised and have no rights, women are still being body shamed in media, and beaten up in their homes feeling guilty for having provoked someone, raped and told they dressed like a slut. What can I do to change any of this?

I feel like it's our responsibility together to start making noise, taking action. We need to have a more 'fight it' attitude, get angry, make some waves, be loud. There's absolutely been progression but we don't want to take two steps forward and then one step back. I personally think our generation has sat back a bit, because we could, which is awesome, but let's not let that slip! …

So host your own girl gang meetings. Make a poster/flag, ask any girl or feminist guy you think is cool, wanna be friends with, that wants to be part of it, to come. Be inclusive, extend the friendship group, create a safe environment and be vulnerable with each other. Exchange emails and discuss what you do, what you want to do, what you need help doing and anything you feel passionately about, injustices, prejudices and things you want to change. We need to share information to find out what needs changing. Let's inform each other. And please, I urge you, have a political opinion.

Kate Nash

GOODBYE TO GOOD GIRLS

Phoebe Hamilton-Jones

We are shaped, in large part, by all the women we know when we're young. I love Virginia Woolf's words, 'we think back through our mothers if we are women'. And I suppose that my early childhood feminism was founded on the sensitive, ambitious, creative, audacious women I was surrounded by as I grew up. Women who painted their apartments teal and bold yellow, women who told me not to duck compliments, who spoke about menstruation (God forbid!) at dinner parties, who assumed that work and children were equally, joyfully important, who forged their exciting high-flying careers in the arts and in business. I was, and am, shy, but watching these outspoken and passionate women filled me with courage. I think I was attracted, in part, to feminism's ability to shock, its dark humour. There is something very depressing about fitting into people's expectations.

This nirvana was not to last. We began to meet with overt sexism in our daily lives – from street harassment (which we found happened more when we were in our school uniforms than not), to our fathers always being handed the bill in the restaurant, to the hyper-sexualisation of women in music videos, to the rarity of seeing black women as the 'cover girl', to the comedy panels dominated by men, to Page Three. These fragments of sexism mounted and became stifling. And they were aggravated by the frustrating complacency among many we knew who felt that gender equality had been achieved, the battles won.

Then when we were sixteen we became aware of several cases within and outside of our friendship group of physical abuse and online sexual bullying by boys, and I remember being very shocked. I have no doubts about the links between violent gonzo porn and abusive relationships. I think many of us turned to, or confirmed, our feminism after this.

And so aged sixteen, after an afternoon of heated discussion, my friend Clara Bennathan and I decided to found FemSoc. The reaction at school was really heartening – staff and pupils got behind it from the start, sending us articles, blogs, ideas. It clearly came at a time when many of us wanted a forum dedicated to debating these issues and a place to be active.

Now our FemSoc meets weekly to explore key feminist issues including positive discrimination, sexism embedded in language, the role of men in feminism, intersectionality, the male gaze in the arts, abortion, and women in the workplace, in music, sport and comedy ... We try where we can to propose viable solutions, from overhauling the structure of the working day to suit childcare or finding smart rebuffs to street harassment. If a roomful of teenagers on a sleepy Monday lunchtime can come up with suggestions to improve women's lives, it is clearly possible for MPs, business managers, army generals and so on to adjust the patriarchal structures and promote gender equality within their sectors of society. What is lacking is the will, the recognition of sexism as a problem and the belief that greater change is possible, persistence key. Through FemSoc we have run campaigns, written articles, visited Parliament as part of Young Minds Charity to raise awareness about sexual pressures on young people, and organised a major cross-generational forum with, as panellists, Juliet Stevenson, Jessica Quarshie, Naomi Alderman and Meg Rosoff.

Our membership is seventy strong and all women, because I am at an all-girls school. I believe very strongly in men's participation in feminism but I also believe in the importance of all-female spaces and activist groups (which are very different from all-male enclaves, be they elitist golf clubs or drinking societies, because women still start from a disadvantaged position.) All-women spaces are practical, providing environments where women can speak and their voices are not drowned out by lower male tones. Women get things done on their own! I believe it's valid to build women's networks and provide a safe place from which to set sail.

I look back to Greenham Common or even to those mythological Amazons. That sense of a community is empowering when we realise just how many of us there are. I like feeling that I belong to a long history and to the breadth of women across the world today. I like feeling drawn into what Woolf calls 'the shelter of a common femininity'.

I often go to the women's ponds on Hampstead Heath; I feel unselfconscious, cradled in the hum of women's voices. We don't know each other and yet we share this stretch of grass, warmed by the sun. So I'll smile at the old woman leaning against a tree in the dusk, her hair curled round in a colourful turban of towel, sitting topless, reading the newspaper.

In our last whole-school assembly I told a story about my great-great-grandmother; she was Spanish, sent to England to marry. When her eldest son died in the First World War she was distraught; her husband committed her to an asylum. She was locked up for the rest of her life because she had refused to grieve quietly. Would an unstable and distressed father have had so little control over his fate? And would society have been able to ignore him as easily as they did her?

I believe that female friendship, female voices and support are fundamental to our power as women. The international sisterhood is a strong force. At a local level there are now feminist societies being established at schools across London. And Clara and I are handing FemSoc over to two year elevens, confident that it will shift and grow.

In a very small way we hope that our FemSoc has shaped the outlook of girls in the years below, and at the very least encouraged them to question the subtle but sinister sexism which pervades our lives today.

I have observed that male writers tend to get asked what they think and women what they feel. In my experience, and that of a lot of other women writers, all of the questions coming at them from interviewers tend to be about how lucky they are to be where they are – about luck and identity and how the idea struck them. The interviews much more seldom engage with the woman as a serious thinker, a philosopher, as a person with preoccupations that are going to sustain them for their lifetime.

Eleanor Catton

. . . if you are a writer, to be a woman is simply to provide a stick to be beaten with . . . if you are a young woman they indulge you with an amused wink. If you are old, they bow to you respectfully. But lose the first bloom of youth and dare to speak before acquiring the respectable patina of age: the whole pack is at your heels!

Simone de Beauvoir, Force of Circumstance

Indeed, I would venture to guess that Anon, who wrote so many poems without singing them, was often a woman.

Virginia Woolf, A Room of One's Own

7

WHAT'S IN A WORD?

Martha Mosse

Perhaps it was because I was fortunate enough to be raised in a home where the principles of feminism were present every day and in everything* that I didn't begin to identify as a feminist until my first year at university. It was here, studying art, that I started to explore whether being labelled – by gender, sexuality, religion, country of birth or residence, politics – was a positive or a negative thing. I threw myself into the self-expression of performance art, where I created solo and group performances of female

* My mum, Kate Mosse, is a best-selling author and the co-founder of the Bailey's Women's Prize for Fiction (née the Orange Prize), the UK's only literary prize honouring women's writing from all over the world, any nationality, any country of residence, any genre, any ethnicity. As well as taking her surname when they married, my dad worked part-time so she could concentrate on building her career. They raised my brother Felix and me together.

bodies writhing grotesquely behind spandex. My performance art practice was an analysis of the labels 'slut', 'spinster', 'mother' and 'perfect'.

For two hours at a time, I danced inside my Spandex prison, depicting an inhuman form attempting to escape the limitations of a label. Reactions to the work were varied and various. A post-show conversation that sticks in my mind was during my residency at a Notting Hill gallery: an audience member praised the work's intent as an honest look at societal pressures, but when I mentioned it was a feminist piece he became extremely hostile. In his hostility he tried to convince me that actually what women really want is to marry a rich man, live off his wealth and never have to work again. I was taken aback by his U-turn – the word 'feminist' had put us on opposite sides of the fence.

Track forward and it's now December 2013. I'm standing nervously offstage at the Grand Connaught Hotel in Covent Garden, about to open the first TEDx Covent Garden Women. Among others speaking that day were Gerardo Porteny, the founder of HeForShe (the campaign now spearheaded by Emma Watson), anti-FGM activist Leyla Hussein, and the founder of #theEveryday Sexism Project and fellow contributor to this book Laura Bates. For the first time since leaving home, I was introduced to a whole wider audience of people who called themselves feminists.

Two years on and the world seems a very different place to

me. Feminism is no longer niche; it is spoken about in newspapers, magazines, online and between friends. The public get behind campaigns to fight misogyny in the media (remember Protein World – ARE YOU BEACH BODY READY?!). Initiatives like the Everyday Sexism Project give women from all over the world and from any background the opportunity of a voice; my fourteen-year-old cousin is going on a march to protest against the media using women's bodies as a commodity to sell; celebrity supermodels (Karlie Kloss's coding for girls), singers (Beyoncé's notorious 'Feminist' signage) and actors (Emma Watson's HeForShe activism) are encouraging young girls to expect more from life, to go for what they want to achieve and not let themselves be held back, or hold themselves back, because they are female.

Despite all this, it seems there is a stigma around the term. Is it more limiting than encouraging? Does it hinder change rather than accelerate it? In a modern society, where all of my male friends live their lives according to feminist principles – though would probably never identify as feminists – what is it about the *word* that makes people so angry? I'm not talking about ideas, or what it stands for; what it means or how it has evolved. Simply the word itself? The label has served for many generations, trying to represent all views fairly under the umbrella of equality of opportunity and fairness. But, as more and more people seem to be embracing the values and empowerment of feminism, has the label passed its sell-by date?

People find the broadness of the term annoying – they are irritated by its attempt to encompass so many views and identities at once. Parts of the world have changed considerably since the Suffragists and Suffragettes were fighting for the vote in the early years of the twentieth century; societal expectations of men and women have changed, in terms of work, independence, freedoms and attitudes. Has the word not kept pace with these changes? In the past fifty years there have been several feminist movements, with different key values at the heart of them – but all identifying as feminist. Andrea Dworkin is different from Gloria Steinem, Angela Davis from Nawal el Saadawi, but they are all feminists.

Since exploring these issues through activism and art, I've come to the conclusion that it matters as much as it ever did to define myself as a feminist. The simple truth is that however things have improved for some women, the world does not offer equal opportunities to women and men. Everywhere, girls and women are still objectified, intimidated and harassed on the street. Women's bodies are still used to advertise anything from cars to food to computers. In many countries women are still under-represented in politics, media, sport. In the UK, women are paid 78 per cent of their male colleagues' wage for work of equivalent value. And in some places in the world it is illegal for women to drive or to vote. Women and girls are forced into sex and underage marriage, are not allowed to learn to read or to go to school, are subjected to FGM and live in constant fear of sexual assault or rape.

I call myself a feminist because I am proud of what feminists have done. Proud of the women of the past from all over the world who have campaigned and fought for the benefit of those coming after them. I call myself a feminist because I believe women deserve to be treated equally to men. I call myself a feminist so that friends may think twice before repeating a rape joke – or laughing at one. I call myself a feminist because, for me, the word embodies strength, courage, loyalty and determination.

Feminism is liberation from the constraints of society; it is to exist as you wish and to feel you can achieve anything. Feminism releases women – and men – to live the lives we want to, to make a contribution to our society in the way that suits our abilities and energies, not restrictions laid down by gender or race or class.

Feminism is fairness.

And then, perhaps, when the world does achieve equality, we will need no labels at all.

The truth will set you free, but first it will piss you off.

Gloria Steinem

[Equality] is not a concept. It's not something we should be striving for. It's a necessity. Equality is like gravity, we need it to stand on this earth as men and women, and the misogyny that is in every culture is not a true part of the human condition. It is life out of balance, and that imbalance is sucking something out of the soul of every man and woman who's confronted with it. We need equality, kinda now.

Joss Whedon

I call myself a feminist. Isn't that what you call someone who fights for women's rights?

The Dalai Lama

WHY I CALL MYSELF A FEMINIST

Meltem Avcil

Many Kurds have fled from all over the Middle East due to the civil war against them. My family is among them. We fled from Turkey to England and applied for asylum. Most governments, including in the UK, understand the conflict that goes on in Iraq, Iran, Syria and Turkey against the Kurds but have a hard time believing in the applicants for asylum as there are thousands who claim to be Kurdish but are not. Despite all the evidence we provided, we still had to wait for six years before being locked up in Yarl's Wood detention centre for three months while waiting to be deported back to the Middle East. But luckily I had the chance to stay, and live in two different societies.

Middle East. The land of science, mathematics and many

other things. That is where we Kurds come from. Our mothers' hands tell a thousand different stories. Their bent backs are a form of life's appreciation for years of their hard work, their eyes are just as generous and kind as their words. They smell of fresh soil and love. They tie their babies to their backs and work from dawn until sunset. They carry buckets of water to and fro to save the day. And no, there is no payment for any of this. Pay is a husband coming home and expecting more and more. Expecting his wife to give birth, raise the child, dig the soil, work on the farms, carry the water, feed the animals, cook and feed him. At times this woman does receive a payment: that is, her husband taking all his day's frustration out on her by beating her, usually with a belt. This man's pride is as useless as himself. Then there are the ill-fated daughters of this man. They are brought up to not bring shame onto the family.

'Family' meaning just the man himself because he is the only important figure. Their education is to learn how to sit, stand, walk, talk, clean, cook, dig soil, work on the farms, carry water, serve tea and marry. Otherwise, they will be added to the list of beatings and become outcasts. And may God help them if they have a brother. The prince of the house, the one and only, the second breadwinner. He can study, have sex before marriage, drink, drive, have a girlfriend, go abroad and work. Only because he is a male. In this society, the girls are seen as copper whereas the boys are seen as gold. On this land, you can hear the silent cries of the mothers echoing in the mountains. The mothers are creators of this power but they have been left powerless.

This is not to say that every family is like this, but the majority are. And then we have the Kurdish female fighters. Guns in their hands and, still, babies tied to their backs. They have vowed to protect their children, husbands, friends and land. Each bullet that leaves the gun is a victory for these women. Their nights are days and days are nights. They are proud, and from within. They do not leave the room for men to protect them, they stand firm and proud. Believing that if there will be a winner, it will be both women and men. Their alarms are bombs and gunshots. So the last thing they care about is equal pay, because the only job is to become a soldier. Islamic State have said that if they were to be shot by women they would straight away go to hell, and so they should. But this is just one part of the world. I live in two societies: one is the Kurdish and the other is the English.

Belief in the social, economic and political rights of women was taught by English society and that is how I became a feminist. Women should be respected all around the world for they are creators. Not sex objects, fragile beings or powerless, but powerful creators. English society taught me just that. That there is a way forward if both sexes come together and work for actual change.

But here, in England, I have also been introduced to

commercial media always telling girls that they are not good enough. That they should lose weight day in and day out, that they should compete with their own sex to look better and better. Not to use their brains but to use their bodies, not to use their pens but to use their lip-liners. Telling them what to wear: push-up bras, high-waist jeans, crop tops and a million other things. Now of course it is a choice – but many young girls don't know what a choice is. And the same goes for boys too. In music videos, on billboards, in movies and in advertisements they are subconsciously taught that the existence of the opposite sex is only to serve them. And so they enter adulthood with this mentality. Boys too are told what to wear, which gym to go to, which steroids to use, which hairstyle to sport, how to talk and what to think. So we see that both sexes are in this vicious circle of obeying the media constantly. If you look carefully you will see many people striving to be the same yet different.

In this essay I have shown two different worlds and would like to define equality for myself. Equality is simply women being free from men. Meaning women should be free from what men like them to wear, what men like to hear, what men like to eat, what men find sexy, free from how to love a man and finally free from the thought that this is a man's world. No make-up, hair extensions, tight dresses or high heels. Women could learn to love themselves first. Just as they are. Plain and beautiful each holding their own gift. Maybe many of us have not become great inventors because we gave all of our power and thoughts to men. Females have a higher life expectancy than men, so basically we have more time to find our talents and gifts and work on them! Women, you are all creators. No matter who you are or what your circumstances, you have the power to say no and stand up for your own kind of change. Let men try to be equal to you because your worth and value are higher than mountains. If a man tells you that you cannot do it, make sure you do it. You are not the woman who stands behind that great man, you are the creator and therefore the great one. It is time to walk to the front lines. English society has taught me that a woman's education is as important as a man's, that there is a way to be equal. There is a famous saying: 'You educate a man; you educate a man. You educate a woman; you educate a generation.' And the total of all these words is why I call myself a feminist.

A cultural fixation on female thinness is not an obsession about female beauty but an obsession about female obedience. Dieting is the most potent political sedative in women's history; a quietly mad population is a tractable one.

Naomi Wolf, The Beauty Myth

You Don't Have to Be Pretty. You don't *owe* prettiness to anyone. Not to your boyfriend/spouse/partner, not to your co-workers, especially not to random men on the street. You don't owe it to your mother, you don't owe it to your children, you don't owe it to civilization in general. Prettiness is not a rent you pay for occupying a space marked 'female'.

Erin McKean

'But I hate to hear you talking so like a fine gentleman, and as if women were all fine ladies, instead of rational creatures. We none of us expect to be in smooth water all our days.'

Jane Austen, Persuasion

Women are responsible for two-thirds of the work done worldwide, yet earn only 10 per cent of the total income and own 1 per cent of the property ... So, are we equals? Until the answer is yes, we must never stop asking.

Dame Judi Dench, voice-over for an equals.org video

WHAT CAN MEN DO TO SUPPORT FEMINISM?

Reni Eddo-Lodge

It was, perhaps, Ryan Gosling who triggered our recent fascination with feminist men. Five years ago he spoke out against the Motion Picture Association of America's decision to rate his film *Blue Valentine* an X-rated NC-17. That's a rating usually reserved for films like the erotic thriller *Eyes Wide Shut*, or gruesome horror *Saw.* It seemed a little over-cautious for *Blue Valentine*, a film in which a young, working-class couple attempt to repair an unhappy marriage. The MPAA's justification for *Blue Valentine*'s rating was a scene in which Gosling's character performs oral sex on the film's female lead. By comparison, the Association has given less severe age ratings to films that feature women being raped by mutants and lizard men. Frustrated, *Blue*

Valentine's filmmakers appealed against the rating, and Ryan Gosling released a statement in support of the appeal.

'You have to question a cinematic culture which preaches artistic expression, and yet would support a decision that is clearly a product of a patriarchy-dominant society, which tries to control how women are depicted on screen,' Gosling's statement read. He continued: 'The MPAA is okay supporting scenes that portray women in scenarios of sexual torture and violence for entertainment purposes, but they are trying to force us to look away from a scene that shows a woman in a sexual scenario which is both complicit and complex. It's misogynistic in nature to try and control a woman's sexual presentation of self. I consider this an issue that is bigger than this film.'

The internet fizzed with excitement at the prospect of a Hollywood star calling out a 'patriarchy-dominant society'. Soon after, the infamous meme 'feminist Ryan Gosling' was born, finding its home on Tumblr. On any given image of Gosling, text smouldered over the picture with phrases like: 'Hey girl. Demonstrating our love through the purchase of high-priced, environmentally unfriendly goods is not at all indicative of the beautifully unique elements of our relationship.'

Four years later, research from academics at the University of Saskatchewan found that the effect of feminist Ryan Gosling memes actually increased sympathy for feminist sentiment in men, who, in the university's study, found themselves agreeing with statements like 'the workplace is organised around men's oppression of women'. It's clear that the number of men on feminism's side is growing, and questions about where men fit in the movement have grown from a whisper to a shout. Many a famous man has expressed sympathy with the feminist cause – from Aziz Ansari to John Legend, Daniel Radcliffe to Patrick Stewart, and of course Ryan Gosling. But it's not enough for famous men to speak out; for women who have romantic relationships with men, the question of feminist politics becomes even more pertinent.

There are men who call themselves feminist, of course. They go along to feminist conferences and events, and they're always the first to ask a question after a panel debate. Sometimes they seek space in feminist circles, and often they vie for a place in the activism. They desperately want to be heard, or they're busy asking, with earnest eyes, 'What can men do to support feminism?'

The first thing men can do is recognise that they heavily benefit from a society in which women still fight for self-determination. There's an old saying about heterosexual gender relations: 'No one will ever win the battle of the sexes because there's too much fraternising with the enemy.' It elicits a laugh, but it also raises a serious question. How can we cultivate fulfilling relationships whilst being hyper-aware that misogyny stains so much of everyday human interaction? It's simplistic for us, as feminists, to categorise men into the good kind and the bad kind. That's not how the insidious nature of sexism works. For women who date men, the best measure of a straight man's feminism is how he engages in relationships with the women in his life.

Can the feminist man respect that a woman might resist being sexually objectified when the act of objectification takes place without her own sexual agency? Is the feminist man taking up women's space to show his dedication to the cause, or is he using his influence to change his own social spheres in order to make them more feminist? Is he asking the difficult questions about gender disparities in his workplace, or challenging sexist attitudes in his friendship group? That's the hard, socially precarious work, but feminist women do it every day, fully aware of the repercussions. Does he look at feminist women in awe instead of understanding the complex nuances of being a woman? After all, we're not all about strong politics and fearlessness all the time. A feminist man cares for you when you're vulnerable and supports you when you're strong. When BBC Radio's *Woman's Hour* undertook research into domestic labour in the home, they found that women are still doing twice as much housework as men, and that younger couples argue about it the most. While girls are told that housewifery is no longer our only destiny and we are free to reach for the stars, boys aren't being taught to pitch in and do their share.

Recently, I transitioned from vegetarianism to veganism.

Talking with a friend who's looking to go meat-free, I had explained that being vegan isn't an identity, it's more like a process in which you have to retrain yourself to change your habits. Reflecting on our conversation, I realised that this is my approach to feminism too. It's not quite the same as swapping out cow's milk for soy, but it is about creating good habits – doubly so for men who sympathise with feminism but have grown up in a society that tells them they deserve a bit more because they're male. For feminism to succeed, the onus is on men to adapt and change. That means listening, increasing their self-awareness and giving up some space. It requires men to engage with and recognise the importance of care work, seeing the gender disparities and asking what they can do to change them. For men to move with the feminist journey they first need to accept that it's okay to be a supporting character in a woman's life.

We're not agitating for a matriarchy, but a feminist man must consider care work as important as waged work. So often, cleaning and care are considered demeaning, but they are the vital jobs that allow all other work to take place. A model in which women are required to give male partners unconditional support in their lives – relocating for their careers if need be, taking a back seat when required – is unsustainable. A feminist man must realise that this unconditional support is relational, that her needs are as important as his, and that her voice is as legitimate as his. The men I've met, known and loved with the best gender politics don't necessarily declare themselves feminists, but rather demonstrate their commitment to women's liberation through their actions, not just their words.

Now and in the future patriarchal attitudes will benefit no one, least of all the men.

Eva Figes, Patriarchal Attitudes

Unconscious biases hurt women, but they also hurt men ... As feminists, it is our job to call attention to our cultural neuroses about masculinity and femininity.

Siri Husvedt, Fifty Shades of Feminism

Feminism isn't a single issue any more. It is nothing less than a change to history. It is the most fundamental shift in human consciousness since Darwin's natural selection, the recalibration of humanity world-wide. It is a long slow process like the movement of the earth's crust. Like the tectonic plates it will buck and shudder. But it cannot come to an end. It cannot be written off. We are, after all, half the human race.

Joan Bakewell, Fifty Shades of Feminism

It's hard to be told to *lighten up* because if you lighten up any more, you're going to float the fuck away.

Roxane Gay, Bad Feminist

I'd rather regret the things I've done than regret the things I haven't done.

Lucille Ball

BIOGRAPHIES

Isabel Adomakoh Young has just graduated with a BA in English from Trinity College, Cambridge. Her best-selling children's book *Lionboy* toured the world as a Complicité stage show, and she's a founding director of Brainchild Festival. She performs with the drag troupe Pecs, collective Shotgun Carousel and psych-pop band Corinthians. She's an enthusiastic feminist, actress and journalist.

Amy Annette is a writer, performer and producer. In 2015 she worked with Tania Harrison on Latitude Festival and this year she is working on a show called *What Women Want*, looking at misconceptions, misogyny and the masterworks of Helen Hunt. Graduating from Durham University with a degree in politics in 2012, she worked on the Obama campaign before returning to London to work in comedy. Amy has had a hand in producing award-winning shows at the Edinburgh Festival since 2010.

Jade Anouka is an actor and has worked at the RSC, the National, played Juliet and Ophelia at the Globe and Hotspur at the Donmar Warehouse and in New York. Jade received the Stage Acting Excellence Award for her performance in one-woman play *Chef* which she performed at Edinburgh festival and Soho Theatre. Jade also writes poetry; her first collection, *Eggs on Toast*, is out now.

Meltem Avcil is a twenty-one-year-old female, activist of humanity, student, part-time worker and daughter. After being locked up, despite being innocent, at the age of thirteen with her mother in Yarl's Wood detention centre, stripped of her rights, freedom and treated like a criminal, she has decided to take control of her life and follow her passion.

Laura Bates is the founder of the Everyday Sexism Project. She writes regularly for the *Guardian*, *Independent*, *Time* and many others. She received the Georgina Henry Award at the 2015 British Press Awards. Laura's first book, *Everyday Sexism*, was shortlisted for Waterstones' Book of the Year and named one of the *Bookseller*'s Top 10 Non-Fiction Books of the Year 2014.

Emily Benn is a local councillor in the London Borough of Croydon, and was a candidate in the 2015 general election. She was first selected as a candidate for the 2010 election aged seventeen.

Bertie Brandes grew up in Hampstead, north London, and went to the King Alfred School, leaving in 2008 to do a degree in English literature at Queen Mary, University of London. While there she started writing a weekly column for *Vice* called Pretty Girl Bullshit, and took the full-time position of fashion editor once she graduated. She left *Vice* in 2013 and is currently contributing features editor of *i-D* magazine. She also co-founded and edits an independent, ad-free young women's magazine called *Mushpit*.

Rosie Brighouse joined the human rights campaigning organisation Liberty as a legal officer in 2013. She is a solicitor and, before coming to Liberty, worked at a number of firms including Bhatt Murphy Solicitors. She is particularly interested in human rights and the criminal justice system, the rights of people in detention and victims' rights.

Reni Eddo-Lodge is a writer and journalist. She likes social justice and nail polish. Her first book, *Why I'm No Longer Talking to White People About Race*, will be published by Bloomsbury in early 2017.

June Eric-Udorie is a sixteen-year-old girls' rights campaigner and writer. She is an adviser and ambassador for the children's charity Plan UK and sits on the #YouthForChange panel, a group of young people working internationally to end female genital mutilation (FGM) and child marriage in a generation. Her writing has appeared in *Cosmopolitan* online, the *Huffington Post* and the *Guardian* among others, and she is a regular writer for the *New Statesman*. June Eric-Udorie also campaigns against FGM with the youth charity Integrate Bristol. You can find her regularly thinking aloud on Twitter @juneericudorie.

Sofie Hagen is a twenty-six-year-old multi-award-winning stand-up comedian from Denmark. She has appeared on *The Verb* on BBC Radio 3, *Alan Davies Après Ski* on BBC 2 and *Russell Howard's Stand-up Central* on Comedy Central. Sofie blogs for the *Huffington Post* and *Standard Issue* magazine and runs her own podcast *Comedians Telling Stuff*. She was voted Best Newcomer in the Foster's Edinburgh Comedy Awards 2015.

Phoebe Hamilton-Jones was born in London in 1997. She co-founded South Hampstead High School's FemSoc in 2013. A passionate feminist, she's also published stories online, loves reading, sailing, campaigning and theatre. After a gap year she will read English at university.

Maysa Haque is a Canadian prairie girl, pursuing a Bachelors of Arts and Science at McMaster University. After studying abroad in France, she is currently tackling classical Arabic in Jordan. Her interests include languages, Islam, gender studies and feminism. She aspires to become a successful, knowledgeable and productive member of society and to own a pet cat.

Caroline Kent began life as a small town Catholic emo. She discovered feminism on Tumblr and the rest, as they say, is herstory. She performed as a burlesque dancer whilst studying fashion, and now combines writing about sex for national newspapers with a career in marketing.

Abigail Matson-Phippard has been volunteering at her local Rape Crisis Centre for around three years. She volunteers at the drop-in where female survivors of sexual violence can come for emotional support, and with the advocacy team who offer support to survivors surrounding the criminal justice process.

Naomi Mitchison, MEng, MIET, is an electronics engineer, currently working as a senior hardware engineer for Selex ES. A keen promoter of science and technology, she has worked hard to bring engineering to the wider community, a role which won her the Institute of Engineering and Technology's Young Woman Engineer of the Year award in 2015.

Martha Mosse found her feminist voice as a performance artist, and for two years toured the UK with a durational performance analysing the limitations of labels – a practice that culminated in Mosse giving the opening speech at the first TEDx Covent Garden Women. Today Martha works freelance in arts production and is the director of new artistic co-op, THE STRAIN.

Yas Necati is an eighteen-year-old feminist activist and campaigner. She is a team member at No More Page 3 and also campaigns for better sex and relationships education. She loves cats, poetry and brownies. You can find her online at yasnecati.com.

Louise O'Neill grew up in Clonakilty, a small town in West Cork, Ireland, and read English studies at Trinity College Dublin. She then completed a postgraduate diploma in fashion buying from the Dublin Institute of Technology. She moved to New York City in 2010 and spent a year working for *Elle* magazine there. Her debut novel, *Only Ever Yours*, won the *Sunday Independent* Newcomer of the Year at the 2014 Bord Gáis Energy Irish Book Awards, the *Bookseller*'s inaugural YA Book Prize and the Children's Books Ireland Eilís Dillon Award. Her second novel, *Asking For It*, will be published in 2015.

Laura Pankhurst grew up in Hertfordshire, with annual visits to Ethiopia, which is her second home, and has been involved with feminist activism from a very young age. Laura is currently a law student at the University of Cambridge.

Samira Shackle is a freelance journalist who writes on foreign affairs, politics, race and gender. A former *New Statesman* staff writer, she spent a year living and working in Pakistan, and has also reported from India, Bangladesh and Kenya. In 2014 she was named one of MHP's best UK journalists under thirty.

Tania Shew is a third-year history student at the University of Sussex. She was a member of the Camden School for Girls Feminist Club, was part of an advisory group on feminism in education for the charity UK Feminista and sat on the editorial board of the magazine *Feminist Times*.

Alice Stride's first foray into feminist books was with her essay 'Saving the Bush', winner of Virago Press's writing competition for *Fifty Shades of Feminism*. She is one of five children, the legacy of which is talking too fast. She loves cheese and *Desert Island Discs* – ideally at the same time. Alice works for Women's Aid, the national charity to end domestic violence against women and children.

Hajar J. Woodland is a singer and copywriter and lives in London.

Jinan Younis is a theology student at the University of Cambridge. In 2013 she was awarded the Christine Jackson Young Person Award at the Liberty Human Rights Awards for her feminist activism in her school. She has written extensively on issues facing young women at university and hopes to continue working in the field of women's rights.

And from our other two editors:

Rachel Holmes is the author of *Eleanor Marx: A Life*, serialised on BBC Radio 4 Book of the Week and short-listed for the James Tait Black Prize. Her previous books include The *Hottentot Venus: The life and death of Saartjie Baartman* and *The Secret Life of Dr James Barry*. She is Visiting Literary Fellow at Mansfield College, Oxford. Her biography of Sylvia Pankhurst will be published by Bloomsbury in 2018.

Victoria Pepe is an editor and literary scout who lives in London.

ESSAY COPYRIGHT

ACKNOWLEDGEMENTS

Caitlin Moran, *How to Be a Woman* (Ebury Press, 2011)

Mia Hamm

Nora Ephron, Commencement Address for Wellesley College, 1996

Adela Pankhurst, *Rebel Girls: How Votes for Women Changed Edwardian Lives* by Jill Liddington (Virago, 2006)

Chimamanda Ngozi Adichie, *Americanah* (Fourth Estate, 2014)

Shulamith Firestone, *The Dialectic of Sex* (Quill, 1970)

Tina Fey, *Bossypants* (Sphere, 2011)

Katharine Hepburn

Ellen DeGeneres, *Seriously I'm Kidding* (Grand Central Publishing, 2011)

Marian Anderson

Roseanne Barr

Natasha Walter, *Living Dolls* (Virago, 2010)

Malala Yousafzai, the *Guardian*, 25 August 2014

Kate Mosse, the *Huffington Post,* 19 September 2014

Jenny Eclair, the *Scotsman,* 24 May 2011

Sarah Millican, *Dave's One Night Stand*, 2010, reproduced by kind permission

E. Lockhart, *The Disreputable History of Frankie Landau-Banks* (Disney-Hyperion, 2009)

Maya Angelou, *Rainbow in the Cloud* (Virago, 2014)

Susie Orbach, *Fat is a Feminist Issue* (Arrow, 1978), reproduced by kind permission of The Random House Group Ltd

Charlotte Church, John Peel Lecture 2013, reproduced by kind permission

Jo Clifford, playwright, www.teatrodomundo.com, reproduced by kind permission. Extract from her talk at the Edinburgh International Book Festival event 'Why I Call Myself A Feminist', 30 August 2015

Paris Lees, the *Guardian*, 18 January 2013

Gloria Steinem, reproduced by kind permission

Kathleen Hanna, interview with Jacki Lydon, www.npr.org, 2014 (National Public Radio)

Kimberlé Crenshaw, 'Mapping the Margins: Identity Politics and Violence Against Women of Color' from *The Public Nature of Private Violence,* edited by Martha Albertson Fineman and Roxanne Mykitink (Routledge, 1994)

Rebecca West

Claire Messud, interview with Jacki Lydon, www.npr.org, 2013

Katharine Hepburn

Mary Wollstonecraft, *A Vindication of the Rights of Woman* (Joseph Johnson, 1792)

G. D. Anderson

Amy Poehler, *Yes Please* (Picador, 2014)

Jessica Valenti, *Full Frontal Feminism: A Young Woman's Guide to Why Feminism Matters* (Seal Press, 2007)

Bridget Christie, *The List* (22 July 2014), reproduced by kind permission

Tina Fey, *Bossypants* (Little, Brown, 2011)

Charlotte Perkins Gilman, *Women and Economics* (Small, Maynard & Company et al, 1898)

Annie Lennox, *Cosmopolitan*, 7 March 2012

Maya Angelou

Margaret Atwood, quoted by Margaret Joe, Yukon Legislature, 5 December 1990, Hansard

Mary Shelley

Marianne Moore, 'Roses Only', *Complete Poems* (Faber & Faber, 2003)

Sandi Toksvig, the *Guardian*, 6 December 2009

Mindy Kaling, *Is Everyone Hanging Out with Me?* (Ebury Press, 2011)

Mae West

Charlotte Brontë, *Jane Eyre* (Smith, Elder and Company, 1847)

Marina Keegan, *The Opposite of Loneliness* (Simon and Schuster, 2014) Copyright © 2014 by Tracy and Kevin Keegan. All rights reserved. Reproduced by kind permission of Scribner, a Division of Simon & Schuster, Inc.

Toni Morrison, *Home* (Chatto and Windus, 2012)

L. M. Montgomery, *Anne of Green Gables* (M. A. and W. A. J. Claus, 1908)

North American fairy tale, *Angela Carter Book of Fairy Tales* (Virago, 2005)

Jeanette Winterson, *Oranges are Not the Only Fruit* (Pandora Press, 1985), extract reproduced by kind permission of Peters Fraser & Dunlop (www.petersfraserdunlop.com) on behalf of Jeanette Winterson

Malala Yousafzai, the *Guardian*, 7 October 2013

Susie Orbach, *Fat is a Feminist Issue* (Arrow Books, 1978), reproduced by kind permission of The Random House Group Ltd

Sojourner Truth, 'Ain't I a Woman?', *Truth's Narrative*, 1875

Michelle Obama, G20 Summit speech to pupils at Elizabeth Garrett Anderson School, Islington, London, 2 April 2009

Joseph Gordon-Levitt, *Ellen: The Ellen Degeneres Show*, 9 January 2014

Michelle Horton, www.parenting.com, www.mom.me, www.EarlyMama.com, reproduced by kind permission

Amy Poehler, *Yes Please* (Picador, 2014)

Mary Wollstonecraft, *Maria, or The Wrongs of Women* (William Godwin, 1798)

Michelle Horton, www.parenting.com, www.mom.me, www.EarlyMama.com, reproduced by kind permission

Waris Dirie, Desert Flower Foundation speech www.desertflowerfoundation.org.en

Amy Schumer, Gloria Awards and Gala speech, May 2014

Margaret Atwood, *The Robber Bride* (Virago, 1994)

Cornelia Otis Skinner

Donald McPherson, *CNN*, 7 March 2013

Roxane Gay, *Bad Feminist* (Corsair, 2014)

Elif Shafak, 'Lazy Summer Afternoon', *Fifty Shades of Feminism* (Virago, 2013)

Maya Angelou, *Letter To My Daughter* (Virago, 2008)

E. Lockhart, *The Disreputable History of Frankie Landau-Banks* (Disney-Hyperion, 2009)

Kate Bolick, *Spinster* (Corsair, 2015), reproduced by kind permission

Chimamanda Ngozi Adichie, *We Should All Be Feminists* (Fourth Estate, 2014)

Doris Lessing, *The Golden Notebook* (Grafton, 1973)

Louisa May Alcott, *Little Women Wedded* (Sampson Low, Marston & Co, 1942)

Erica Jong, *Fear of Flying* (Grafton, 1974)

Jessica Valenti, *Full Frontal Feminism: A Young Woman's Guide to Why Feminism Matters* (Seal Press, 2007)

Oxford Online Dictionary, www.oxforddictionaries.com/definition/english/virago

Kate Nash, katenash.tumblr.com, reproduced by kind permission

Eleanor Catton, the *Guardian*, 16 October 2013

Simone de Beauvoir, *Force of Circumstance* (André Deutsch, 1965)

Virginia Woolf, *A Room of One's Own* (Hogarth Press, 1929)

Gloria Steinem, reproduced by kind permission

Joss Whedon, 'Equality Now' speech, 15 May 2006

The Dalai Lama, International Freedom Award acceptance speech, Memphis, United States, 23 September 2009

Naomi Wolf, *The Beauty Myth* (Chatto and Windus, 1990)

Erin McKean, 'You Don't Have to Be Pretty', 20 October 2006, www.dressaday.com

Jane Austen, *Persuasion* (John Murray, 1818)

Dame Judi Dench, voice-over for the equals.org video marking International Women's Day, featuring Daniel Craig and directed by Sam Taylor-Wood, 5 March 2011

Eva Figes, *Patriarchal Attitudes* (Virago 1978)

Siri Husvedt, 'Underground Sexism', *Fifty Shades of Feminism* (Virago, 2013), reproduced by kind permission

Joan Bakewell, 'If I Couldn't be a Man', *Fifty Shades of Feminism* (Virago, 2013), reproduced by kind permission

Lucille Ball